BREAKING THE MOLD

Finding Healing After Sexual Abuse

ROSALEE KIDD-MIGHTY

BREAKING THE MOLD. Copyright © 2023. Rosalee Kidd-Mighty. All Rights Reserved.

Printed in the United States of America.

No portion of this book may be reproduced, stored in a retrieval system, or transmitted in any form or by any means, except for brief quotations in printed reviews, without the prior written permission of DayeLight Publishers or Rosalee Kidd-Mighty.

ISBN: 978-1-958443-53-8 (paperback)

Dedication

This book is dedicated to RGM and all the women who have shared their sexual abuse story with me, as well as all those women who have lost their fight, joy, voice and Purpose to pain and hurt, and especially from sexual abuse. Know that there is one who hears, sees and knows all, the Lord God Almighty, so you are never alone!

Acknowledgements

Love, praise and thanksgiving pour out from me to my Abba Father, the One true God. Thanks be to you, for without you I wouldn't have survived, and be empowered to pen my story to help to heal hurting hearts.

To my extraordinary husband Doyle, I am grateful for your support, love, and encouragement all these years. Thanks to you and our amazing daughter for 'cutting me some slack' and allowing me more 'sleepy time' as I write this book.

I am truly grateful to Jackie, Nadine, Kimoy, Yvonne, Leonia, Geraldine, and Expectant Crew members who encouraged and covered me in prayers as I wrote.

Authors Renate McDonald and Colleen Turner McGregor, thanks for giving insights and tips unselfishly for the completion of my book.

Geraldine Price, you took the time to edit my book and provide solace and sound advice, God bless you. I am truly grateful. You were my Life Group Leader, but I consider you a lifeline, wonderful prayer support and an extraordinary encourager, keep on touching lives.

Kimoy, what can I say, you are truly a rare gem, one of the kindest, loving, authentic persons I know. Your passion to please HIM is extraordinary and infectious. Thanks for all the help you provided as I wrote.

Crystal Daye of DayeLight Publishers Limited, thanks for the coaching, encouragement, teachings and sound advice, you have made writing simpler. Big up to my Reach Millions cohort four (4), thanks for the encouragement, love and being a sounding board for my book.

For all my prayer partners, I have penned my thanksgiving in chapter 11, I am truly blessed to have each of you in my life.

Table of Contents

Dedication iii
Acknowledgements v
Introduction 9
Foreword 11
Preface 15
Chapter 1: History—My Roots 19
Chapter 2: Don't tell anybody, or else!! 27
Chapter 3: Driva Don't Stop at All Till Yu Reach Town....Kingston!! 35
Chapter 4: Puppy love & school in town 43
Chapter 5: The long-term impact of being sexually abused and near-death experiences 55
Chapter 6: I have decided to follow Jesus....no turning back 61
Chapter 7: Work, the process of being faithful 67
Chapter 8: Anticlimax – my 18th birthday! 79
Chapter 9: The devil is a liar....now I am married 89
Chapter 10: I was married......., now what? 103
Chapter 11: Destiny Helpers 119

Chapter 12: This is not the end but the beginning 135

Introduction

Do you feel like you are a hamster running cycles on a wheel? Are you sick and tired of being sick and tired? Have secrets so hidden that not even your best friend knows them?

I can help you, yes me! I was stuck in a mold but now I'm free. "What does she know about being stuck?", you may ask. Well, I am more than qualified to help you. My childhood was plagued by numerous sexual abuses from as early as four years old until a few days before my eighteenth (18th) birthday; which caused me to be fearful, sad, angry, doubtful and have self-defeating thoughts, like suicide. I am sharing my story (Firstly) to encourage you that you are not the only one struggling with secrets, doubts, and fears fueled by your past of sexual abuse or other trauma. (Secondly), I don't want you to continue in the same mold any longer. Why cope when you can have hope?

One of the steps I took in becoming unstuck is to share my secrets. Now let me share one with you. I can remember having intense mood swings - happily laughing for one moment then in the snap of a finger feeling negative emotions like sadness, anger, timidity, etc. It got so bad that in the early stages of marriage my husband considered separation. His thoughts of moving on with someone else was a wakeup call.

Whew! There, I told you one of my secrets...but it doesn't stop at just telling.

So, come alongside me as I share more secrets, encouragements, food for thought, and how God helped me to break the mold of childhood sexual abuse and find healing.

"For it's not by my power or might but by the Spirit of The Lord God Almighty!"

Foreword

"**D**id you know that according to the Jamaica Gleaner, between January and March 2021 five hundred and sixty-five (565) sexual abuse cases in children were reported?".

Having experienced and overcome child sexual abuse, Rosalee Kidd-Mighty can speak to the devastating effects of sexual abuse which started from the tender age of four (4) years old. She strongly believes that no one, regardless of age, should have to experience the devastating effects of sexual abuse.

It is with this strong belief, commitment and determination, that Rosalee Kidd-Mighty has decided to become a part of the mission and advocacy against the rising incidences of child sexual abuse in Jamaica.

In this Book, **"Breaking the Mold: Finding Healing After Sexual Abuse"**, she has chronicled her own story of personal experiences, and her journey through sexual abuse, highlighting in an unusually "brutally frank and honest manner", some of those moments, and the very deep and intense physical, mental, emotional, and psychological challenges that arose during and after the abuses.

What is captivating to a Reader reading this Book, is how Rosalee Kidd-Mighty doesn't lose sight of who is her true and real ''Destiny Helper'', the Most High God, through Jesus Christ, and empowered by the Holy Spirit working in and through her life and journey with supporters and naysayers whom she calls her ''Destiny Helpers''.

Throughout the Book, despite going through the devastating elements on her journey, Rosalee maintained her focus on ''her mission'', and this is borne out by her occasional 'restlessness' when she wasn't being engaged in activities that would lead her towards achievement. This is one of the strong and impactful points for me throughout the Book, up to and including its ending.

Her journey is interspersed with some anecdotes, Jamaican creole, 'patois', her resilience, beliefs, and unwavering faith despite not always understanding some of the messages from God. These factors allow the Reader to see how balancing the negatives and positives in life can ''work together for good'', all in line with the Promises in Word of God, which is the spiritual foundational doctrine and truth by which she lives.

Her ''Encouragement tips'' to readers, after the challenging moments she experienced, are practical and relatable, and serve to help with the working-through, working-out, and healing processes, as part of God's purpose for her life, and undoubtedly for so many of us to believe - ''He's not done with you yet''!!

That's why I appreciate and am inspired by ''Breaking the Mold: Finding Healing After Sexual Abuse'', and it is my pleasure and joy to recommend it to you.

Mrs. Geraldine Price

Preface

Do you know parents have an important role of speaking prophetically into their children's lives? My Father, at age four (4) "Dada" did just that with his prophetic, unforgettable statement: *"Rosalee is going to turn out to something good and you won't regret it"*. This prophecy set the stage for my greatness as well as Dada naming me 'Afreca' which means African Princess, I am indeed his Princess and My Eternal Fathers' Princess. These prophecies have come true, I have turned out to something good amidst my trials and 'both' my Fathers haven't regretted creating me. They have encouraged me to write.....but write what?

As a child growing up and going through some horrendous experiences, I enjoyed creating stories in my head and writing others down. I even envisioned writing my life story, but at the time I didn't know what I was going to write about so the pages were blank......

I never would have thought I would be sharing deep dark secrets about my sexual abuse for the world to hear and see. Yet as an adult, whenever I have been called upon by the Holy Spirit to speak.....share my story, at first, I was fearful....but the constant result was that lives were ALWAYS changed, Glory to God!!!.

Then in July of this year, 2023, I attended an enlightening Writers' Workshop, 'Reach Millions Author Live 2023, hosted by Crystal Daye of Dayelight Publishers. At the workshop the Holy Spirit revealed to me that I was to write MY STORY instead of a Children's book which I had envisioned. I was excited, yet nervous and fearful of exposing my heart, but in obedience I started the journey of writing.

This book is penned by the Holy Spirit through me, and for such a time as this, a time to encourage hurting women to get up and live out their God-given Purposes. You may be struggling with sexual abuse, infertility, sickness, fear, doubts, silence, self-imposed restrictions, suicide or other self-defeating thoughts, but there is hope. Yes, there is hope in Jesus, and you must know and believe that you are never alone; many women have, and are having these issues, and will trod this same path. Let me assure you that it's not your fault, this life of pain isn't your Purpose; you were created for much more than this, and my prayerful encouragements are the ray of hope you have been seeking.

I too was shrouded in darkness because of sexual abuse which started as early as age four until a few days before my eighteenth birthday. These episodes were not my only pain, I struggled with gripping fear, low self-esteem, rejection, people-pleasing, pride, sickness, infertility and many more. Through the love and direction of the Holy Spirit, I had to fight hard to break these mindsets and walk in my God-given

Purpose. Friend, it was not easy, but with God's help you too can achieve, because you ''can do all things through Christ who strengthens you'', (Philippians 4:13).

So come journey with me as I share through my riveting story as well as prayerful encouragements about how I broke the mold and found healing after sexual abuse. Take my hand and let us break mold together, as our stories aren't finished yet, and with God All things are possible!

Chapter 1

History-My Roots

History

Marcus Mosiah Garvey, one of Jamaica's national heroes, says: "A people without the knowledge of their past, history, origin, and culture, is like a tree without roots."

I grew up hearing everyone being called by their given name or a nickname, so I refer to my mother by the name ''Sonia'', as she was called, and not to be disrespectful in any way to her and her role in my life. As I grew older, this reference to her has continued to date, and she has never responded to me as if she felt disrespected or was offended.

Growing up, the immediate family members comprised of my Father, affectionately called 'dada', my mother ''Sonia'', my older brother Kevin, and myself, all of us living in the same house. My eldest sister, Sophia, my mother's first child before her relationship with my father, lived with my mother's mother, whose name is Violet and affectionately called "Aunt Vie'. The houses were about two houses apart, but based on lots of trees between the houses, referred in Jamaican terms as ''bush'', it gave the appearance of being about ten houses apart. The ''bush'' has significance to my story as will be seen later.

I recall that my relationship with my mother ''Sonia'' during my very early years was pleasant enough, however, as I grew older what I can clearly remember were the ''beatings'' she would administer to Sophia, Kevin and myself, but especially to me. As I aged though, I started to understand her more, also about some of her own childhood challenges which included having to take care of her younger siblings, getting pregnant at an early age, these were all aggravated by my father's not so good treatment of her at times. I then understood why we became targets and witnessed her display of bouts of crying because the frustration and stress were at very high levels.

After I had the great fortune and privilege of accepting Jesus Christ as my personal Lord and Saviour at the age of seventeen (17) years, I came to forgive her for the things she had said to us and the beatings we received. I also met with her one day and we shared our hearts together, and that helped my understanding level and the forgiveness process. She also gave her heart to the Lord Jesus Christ, and now we communicate with prayers and voice notes almost every morning, and she continues to intercede for the entire family.

I remember the day I heard her say she loved me, and was so shocked, but so very pleased to hear those words coming from her lips. Truly, the Lord is to get all glory for that!

My Father was a Farmer, a mason, and was skilled in many other areas including building houses. One of his skills was manifested in building a a machine to crush canes and extract the juice, a feat that left me in awe as I enjoyed the juice so many times. As a little girl my "Dada" would help me with my homework and reading and was one of my main encouragers who told me that I "was bright", and that I was going to do well. I loved him, and when I awoke in the mornings I would run into his arms, and he would ask me what I dreamt about. At bath times he would bathe me, and completed the bath by "stretching me", yes, this is an act whereby after bathing a baby, the child would be held by each hand and each leg, and by the head, at intervals, and bounced up and down, to stretch the limbs and muscles so the child would get taller.

On the funny side, Sophia, who was four years older than I was, would watch intently, and one day she tried to mimic my father. Let's just say I didn't fare out well with this trial as I ended up with what we Jamaicans called "coco" (a bump on my head).

Despite being a loving and caring father, my "Dada" was very strict, and oftentimes became very angry and bitter, primarily towards my mother "Sonia". He demonstrated these emotions in ways that were not at all pleasant, such that he and "Sonia" eventually parted ways. I recall witnessing some of those unpleasant and dangerous moments. Not only did ''Sonia'' experience ''Dada's'' anger, but I too can also recall some moments in my childhood when, at about age seven (7), without asking questions about what he thought he saw or heard, he beat me mercilessly, to the extent where I had cuts and bruises all over my body. The words ''I am sorry'' was never uttered from his lips, neither to me nor to ''Sonia''. After that severe beating, my mother decided to send me to live with grandma, Violet.

Over the years during childhood, and even as an adult, I tried to know and understand my father's heart, but I only got stone-walled, and when he was even slightly receptive to talking, it was always about what ''Sonia'' had done. I dreaded going to look for him or to collect anything, and on one occasion, being an adult then, I told him that I wanted to learn more about him, but he said he just wanted to ''let sleeping dogs lie''. I was crushed but tried to make the most of our visits, always praying for his salvation. There was a time when I pondered whether I should become my father's main caregiver, and the impact it could have on my marriage. After discussing it with my husband, I decided to cry out to God for direction and peace, pointing out to Him that although it was a desire of my heart, I am mindful of it being a possible detriment to my own marital relationship, therefore it's according to His will, not mine. I felt and received the peace that only God can give, so I released my father's care into His capable hands. The Lord God responded to my prayer when I got a call five minutes afterwards informing me that my father had passed away.

It was the year 2016 that my ''dada'' died. Before he died, he was hospitalized because his breathing was shallow as he loved to smoke what he termed his 'friend ganja'. Thankfully, when I picked him up from the hospital en route to his home, I got the opportunity to lead him to Jesus Christ, and he accepted the call.

As an adult, as I gradually learned to talk about my childhood issues and challenges, I chose to forgive my dad, discovering and recognizing that he too had a rough childhood with his dad also being very strict, and unfortunately, as it is said, ''hurting people, hurt people''. That's why it's so important to talk about your hurt to someone you trust or a counsellor, so that (1) you will see things differently, (2) learn to forgive and cope as you 'do this life', (3) bring closure to your hurt.

Roots

My ''roots'' recollections start from age four (4) years. I can remember having conversations with God at that early age. You may ask, why so early? Simply put, I grew up around God-fearing people, as well as born-again Christians. ''Dada's'' mom, affectionately called "Cousin Isie" and Grandma Violet, took me to church when I was young, as well as when I was older and visited.

At age four I had moved to Kingston to live with ''Sonia's'' eldest sister Velma, whom I eventually considered to be my mom. Aunt Velma was an ardent Christian and she; Sophia and I went to church twice on a Sunday (including Sunday school) and for Bible study on Wednesdays. Inasmuch as I was bored at times in the service, I dared not behave restless, as this wasn't allowed, a far cry different from today where children are armed with gadgets to entertain them, even in Church. Growing up in Brooklyn Road, St. Mary, I recall attending a basic school, Miss Kidd's Basic school, and I literally hated going there because of the ''unprovoked and unnecessary beatings'' that were meted out to me and other students. My most pleasant times were romping with my school friends until I was picked up by ''dada'' or ''Sonia''.

I can remember at age seven (7) crying out to God because my classmates were not treating me well. At age eleven (11), I recall bargaining with God just like Gideon, the Judge, did in the Bible, in Judges 6-8. I innocently told God that if He made me pass my Common Entrance exams (An exam that is taken by primary school students to enter high school) I would become a Christian. Well, God kept His end of the bargain, and shamefully I kept mine (six) 6 years later.

Growing up, names were a significant part of this stage of my life, wherein the culture of my hometown was about assigning names that were not always in line with the registered names of persons. I hated all my given names and would literally try to hide when my various names were called, especially the middle and last names. For example, the name ''Rosalee, Afreca Kidd''. Children and even some adults teased me mercilessly, calling me 'kiddy goat', 'goat kid', 'maaaay' (making the sound of a goat). 'Afreca' was changed to 'Africa' and 'a freak' etc. I remember being so hurt I went to my father and asked him why he gave me my names. He assured me by telling me that he named me

'Rosalee' from a rose, 'Afreca' was the name of an African princess in a book he read. I felt a bit better and somehow considered myself a princess.

My name distress did not stop, even in High School, as we read about ''Rosalie Gidharee'' a teenager, who had a wicked character in Michael Anthony's book, Green Days by the River. Again, I was teased without mercy.
Eventually as I got older, I started to embrace my names, and thought that they were very unique..... in the same way that being a child of God makes me unique!!

Encouragement #1

- Don't let your past/history decide your future. It reminds me of God's promise to the Israelites through Isaiah 43:18-19, 18: "Forget the former things; do not dwell on the past". 19: ''See, I am doing a new thing! Now it springs up; do you not perceive it? I am making a way in the wilderness and streams in the wasteland''.

- We can't embrace God and see His future for us if we hold on to our negative past.....Let go...forgive....allow Him to help you. It is not easy but, He alone knows all things and can help you. No! My friend, it is not too late, it is never too late, talk to him now. Father, please help me to.........

Chapter 2

Don't tell anybody, or else!!

Here is my story and my journey......

In 2018, as I lay on the bed experiencing yet another excruciating pain, my legs apart with the doctor and nurse performing a ''pipelle sample'', *(this is the name of the procedure in which a small sample of tissue is taken from the lining of the womb, called the endometrium, and is then sent off to the laboratory to check if there are any cancer or other abnormal cells in the lining of the womb)* my mind flashed over my life with a question, "Why Lord, why yet another painful moment?", as I struggled to hide my tears but not my pain. I then had a vision, in which I could see and hear myself talking to millions of people, encouraging them with my story.

Flash back......to when the pain all began.

Breaking the Mold

The pain all began about age 4, that day I woke up excited for a day of romping with my siblings and friends. My mother was about to leave me in the care of her sister my Aunt Gloria affectionately called Penge (she died many years ago), "Eat your breakfast," she said, "and come up to me at your father's house."

I ate quickly, told Penge I was leaving, and rushed out of the house. As I ran to where the gate was supposed to be (there was no gate), I heard a male voice that I didn't know, calling to me from across the road saying: "Weh yu a guh?" (Jamaican patois for where are you going?) I looked up curiously and with a start, then blurted out, "Sonia seh mi fi come to har at mi fada house." (Sonia said I am to come to her at my father's house). At this time my father was living a few houses away.

After checking the area carefully, the male stranger turned slightly and pointed behind him in the ''bushes'' and said quickly, "Yuh mada deh in desso, mek mi tek yuh to har." (your mother is over there, let me take you to her) I tilted my head thinking aloud, "Mi mada deh ova desso?" He shook his head and said "yes."

I was taught to trust adults but there was a strong unease in my 4 years old stomach. My steps were slow and unsure as I once again enquired if my mother was really over there. I followed this stranger deeper into the bushes. After walking for a while and not seeing my mother, I stopped and said quite outspokenly, "Yuh sure mi mada deh ova yah suh." (Are you sure my mother is here?) He assured me quickly that we would soon see her.

We walked a bit more then he stopped and proceeded to pull down some dried banana leaves and put them on the ground. I enquired urgently, "Weh yu a duh han weh mi mada deh?" (What are you doing and where is my mother?) He replied quickly, "Shet yuh mout han nuh tell nobady weh mi duh cause dem a go beat yuh!" (Shut your mouth and don't tell anybody what I did, because they are going to beat you.)

He pushed me down roughly on the trash, pulled down my underwear and bent over me. I knew something was very wrong, but I couldn't stop it, I was helpless. As I lay there, I felt excruciating pain rushing all through my young body. To this day I don't know what he did and cannot explain it, it's like a block to my conscious mind, and it was only in my twenties that I finally remembered this scene, but not what he did. What I do remember was that (1) as we parted company, he reminded me to be quiet or I would be beaten and (2) how I hurt down there and (3) more hurt when my mother washed my private part.

I went into the house apparently crying and Penge asked if Sonia had chased me away. I quickly grabbed on to that suggestion and nodded yes. She began to pull some of the trash from my body and asked if I had fallen, as I was very dirty, I again shook my head in a yes motion.

Succumbing to my ordeal I fell asleep, only being comforted by sucking my trusted right thumb. I was awakened by my mother's wrath, as she questioned me as to where I was, and announced how disobedient I was. I tried to explain, but didn't know how to do so, remembering the threat from the stranger. Tears flowed as the beatings from my mother soaked literally though my skin, and as a part of me died.

The strange man was partly right, I did get a beating even though I didn't tell, because I wasn't able to explain myself to my mother. More pains gripped my body, and I wept inside as my tortured feminine part burned as "Sonia" bathed me.

At age eight (8) when my other sister, Patrice, and I visited 'Cousin Isie', and where my adult male cousin, *James (I changed his name) also lived. He was chatting with Patrice and I, then he told my sister to go home, which was next door. Again, I knew something was wrong, but I didn't have the strength or knew how to stop it. He proceeded to molest me. I didn't know how to tell him to stop, and I was embarrassed for him and myself. He told me not to tell anyone and gave me more sweets. Patrice had gotten some before she left. Just as he was finished, my father came running through the field, he suspected something was afoot, and searching my face asked me if I was okay and if my cousin had touched me. I averted my eyes, hiding my tears and shook my head indicating that nothing happened.

I was bawling inside, and I knew if I told my dad the truth, he would literally have chopped up my cousin. There is a saying in Jamaica that the people from the parish of St. Mary are ''quick fi draw dem lass" (quick to use their cutlasses/

machetes) and that is so true. Both my mom and dad's side of family knew how to use their cutlasses.

I wish I could tell you that this was the end of my sexual pains, but that wouldn't be true, and I learnt early that "lying doesn't pay". You see, I found myself "lying" so much as a youngster, and for so many reasons, and the unrelenting beatings from Aunt Velma for doing so didn't make that much difference except in the moments..... She would say: (I am laughing as I write this, but it was serious then) "Lulu," as I was affectionately called, "Puss bruk coconat, inna yuh eye", when I would just stare without flinching, into her eyes, and lie blatantly. One day I told her the truth and she didn't believe me, so from then I decided lying wasn't worth it and started telling the truth.

Back to my pain........At New Day All Age School, when I was in Grade 3, one day as I was walking through a packed corridor, I felt a hand grabbing my private parts. As I looked up, I saw an older boy with a lecherous smile on his face passing me. I was mortified, held down my head and rushed to my classroom and cried into my desk. A classmate asked me what had happened to me, and I shook my head, indicating that nothing had happened to me. My teacher was informed that I was crying but again I didn't disclose yet another secret.

When I lived in the Mona area in Kingston, a neighbour's dad would give me money and fondled my breasts. This also happened with a neighbour's granddad when I lived in another area. I would always give my Aunt the monies I got from these persons, but I didn't disclose the dirty secrets when she asked why they gave me the monies.

How I hurt!!, I didn't know who to share my distresses with, or how to share them. I believed and imagined then that this was what God created me for, to be sexually abused. I hated myself for not talking up because I feared repercussions if I did. I would dream about being raped. I felt dirty even at Church as males seemed to undress me with their eyes. I preferred not to look at people and always held my head down.

If you were sexually abused you can identify with me, I had nightmares, I was dreadfully fearful, angry, ashamed, lacked confidence, thought the worst about myself and others, and mistrusted just about everyone and everything.

I remember two instances of mistrust while in High School. One day I was walking to school and a car stopped, the driver and passengers were young men, and one high school girl. They offered me a ride and I politely declined, but they implored me that everything would be fine. I reluctantly climbed in and sat at the edge of my seat praying inwardly and feared they would take me away and rape me.

I silently prayed my thanks to God and sighed with relief as they let me out at my school gate. In our current world I wouldn't have taken the ride, and I would encourage others not to. Why you may ask?, because now that I am walking in confidence with the Lord, I am more trusting now, wiser, and alert, knowing that the Holy Spirit of God is always leading and protecting me. Do I always get things right?, not at all, but it's a process and I am learning to trust God more and more each day of my life, and in every circumstance.

On another occasion some friends and I were returning from a high school trip and the chartered bus had left us because a friend truthfully told the teacher she was waiting on her stepdad to pick us up. Unfortunately, he wasn't able to come so we were stranded. Naturally, my panic mode tripped in, and with much fear, I asked my friend what we were going to do. The other friends laughed at me and just continued enjoying themselves. Their final decision was to 'boom' a ride (hitch a ride) which I was totally against but didn't have another choice.

Several vehicles whizzed past us, but finally a trailer stopped, I was mortified. My friends told the driver where we were going, and we all climbed in. I wanted to jump through the window when the doors closed, and I realized that the cab of the trailer had a bed in it. I instantly imagined us being raped and our bodies discarded. My stomach was in my throat the whole ride, yet my friends were so content and were conversing with the driver. Thank God my fears did not materialize, and we arrived safely in Half-Way-Tree. I really wanted to kiss the ground in praise and thanks but was ashamed of doing so in front of my friends. (smile).

Encouragement #2

- Teach your children to trust their instincts, don't be quick to say they are lying when they share things.

When they speak the truth and we don't believe them, they may think what they felt, saw, and shared, wasn't true and so they may or will keep things inside thinking no one will believe them. They may even share with the wrong persons. It's so very necessary and important to listen to them, investigate, and rely on the Holy Spirit to direct you as you deal with what they have shared.

- Trust your instincts also, it is better to be careful than get hurt. Pray, pray, pray for direction......

Chapter 3

Driva Don't Stop at All Till Yu Reach Town....Kingston!!

As I shared in Chapter 1, Aunt Velma fostered Sophia and myself while we lived in Kingston. She had no children of her own and felt the urge to help her sister "Sonia" who had 4 children at that time, namely, Sophia, Kevin, myself, and Patrice. Elma was born a year later and then George (affectionately called Pete), Jhenielle and Jove whom she had with her late husband, Vincent.

I venture to say, when the Lord has a purpose for your life no one can stop it from being fulfilled, not even you. Sophia didn't want to stay in Kingston, she wanted to return to St. Mary. Aunt Velma was a domestic helper who lived on the premises of her employer (live-in helper), Ernest Upfield, and his family. His family subsequently migrated overseas and so he lived alone. To accommodate Sophia, then me, my Aunt sought approval from her boss to have one more child (first for holidays) living in his home, and he gave his consent. I consider this favour to be a part of God's divine plan, as it's unusual for a boss to allow his helper to foster two of her nieces at his home at which he was a tenant. Mr. Upfield was like an angel to my Aunt and us, a very kind gentleman, and who had no ulterior motive in assisting us.

Sophia had just moved to Kingston before me, and needed a playmate, that's my story and I am sticking to it. (smile). I wasn't the first choice to spend the holidays with her, it should have been Jilly, the younger sister of Velma and Sonia. Unfortunately, Jilly wasn't able to come due to an injury, so I'm grateful that ''the lot" fell bountifully on me.

In order for me to go to Kingston to just spend holidays, my Aunt and mother had to ask ''dada's" permission, and happily he gave his consent. It so happened that at a later date when they asked him if I could live in Kingston he said yes with the unforgettable statement: ***"Rosalee is going to turn out to something good and you won't regret it".***

It was just this year 2023, that I realized this was a prophetic blessing from my father. The *'you won't regret it'* part didn't always entirely seem true due to the many times that I caused my Aunt undue stress because of my curiosity and uniqueness, and at which she sometimes thought of sending me back to St. Mary (smile).

I recall one such time, when I got a lovely red watch which I couldn't read at all because it was an ''analog watch". Being the curious child that I was, I used my teeth to remove the plastic face, played with the little hands and they broke off. I was so shocked and fearful of being severely scolded, that I deceitfully replaced the face and put the watch back in its case. Sadly, my misdeed was discovered when I was all dressed up to go on my first field trip to the Carib Theatre with my School (New Day), to watch a James Bond movie entitled ''Man with the Golden Gun''. Wow!!, talk about bad timing, how am I going to get out of this one, I thought, so I decided that telling the truth was the best thing to do, which I did. Unfortunately, I wasn't expecting the punishment I got, which was: ''Tek aff yu unifarm, yu nah guh again''. (Take off your uniform, you are not going again). Oh no, I thought, now is the time I would have really preferred a beating, as not going to the movie was the worst punishment I could have ever expected or experienced, moreso for telling the truth!!. I hid my tears and reluctantly obeyed my Aunt by taking off my uniform.

I don't remember if I actually prayed, but I believe God stepped in. My Teacher, Mrs. Osbourne was another angel. Not seeing me in the group, she called our home and demanded to know why I wasn't at the pickup point. My Aunt tried explaining my infraction, I wasn't sure what the exact conversation was, but, *all me know sey is dat, mi antie tell mi fi put on back mi uniform faas, faas,* (All I know is that, my Aunt urged me quickly to put my uniforms on again) and so I quickly got dressed, saying: ''Hallelujah! Carib Theatre here I come''. Yes, yes, that to me was indeed a miracle, and I most definitely enjoyed the movie, food, fun and friendship. Did I learn my lesson then, I don't think so but more about my uniqueness later (smile).

I thank God that despite my many escapades, Aunt Velma obeyed Him and didn't send me back to St. Mary. You see dear reader, it wasn't an accident that I came to Kingston instead of my Aunt Jilly. God had a purpose for using my Aunt as part of the destiny journey, as well as for my life and Sophia's.

As I said before, Mr. Upfield was a kind angel and a gentleman. After I spent summer holidays for a while, he seemed to have developed an admiration for me, my uniqueness and being outspoken, nothing sexual. He told my Aunt that I seemed 'bright', and that she was to let me stay....who does this?

We were living under his roof, using his facilities and utilities, and eating his food for free. This could only have been God. I pause here to offer a prayer for Mr. Upfield's family (Mr. Upfield died years ago), ''Lord please bless the Upfield family, wherever they are''!!!

I recall that he would give our Aunt money to purchase store-bought clothes for us, as against clothes made by dressmakers during that era, yes, I know I am dating myself (smile). He also helped to pay school fees for me to attend Waterloo Preparatory School, among other expenses.

He didn't attend Church like my Aunt, but God used him to bless us. Being a 'Jamaican white man', he had his fair share of teasing and speculations about why he was living with his 'black' helper in his house and taking such great care of her nieces. Being teased was the price he paid to accomplish God's purpose for us.

When I was in grade 5, my "safe" world turned upside down, and with this new change I grew up fast. Mr. Upfield's landlady said she needed her house, so, regrettably we all had to seek other living arrangements. Mr. Upfield told my Aunt she could take anything in the house she wanted, and that he had made other living arrangements, so she was to do the same.

This was a very hard time for all of us, because my Aunt had been a live-in helper from, she came to Kingston, and she didn't know any other life. When she sought help from those she knew, most persons said, "A nuh fi yu pickney dem, sen dem ome to dem parents" (These are not your children send them home to their parents). This broke her heart, and one friend named Joan, a friend of Mr. Upfield, encouraged her saying: "Velma, you can do this, get a 'days-worker' job (cleaning homes on a daily basis) and find somewhere to rent to take care of yourself and the girls." My Aunt took her advice and eventually got such a job for a few days.

By divine appointment, a lady from our Church family, named Mrs. Bartley, (God rest her and Mr. Bartley's souls) offered her and us her home to live in because she had vacated it to do some additional works to enhance the structure that was already there. The rent was at a minimal cost.

This was home now but the adjustment took its toll on us, especially me. I was a "foodie", and now I could no longer get the fine foods to which I had become accustomed at Mr. Upfield, like the steaks, hams, oxtail, roast beef, salmon and all the other rich foods. Also, at Mr. Upfield we learned and were exposed to what is called 'fine living', modern etiquette and other social graces.

Additionally, while there, my sister and I shared a room together, but now all three of us had to share a room together, and the meals were what was commonly referred to then as 'poor man food'. Despite these new 'inconveniences' and adjustments, Sophia and I were thankful and grateful because we had a roof over our heads, a clean bed, clothes on our backs, and we never went to bed hungry, but for the love, faithfulness and mercies of God!!!

Encouragement #3

- There is a Jamaican proverbs that says, 'what is fi yuh caan be unfi yuh' which means what is meant for you will be yours. I truly believe that God's purpose will be accomplished in your life as you allow Him to work in and through you, and with you always operating in gratitude and humility.

- I know the encouragement above sometimes this is hard to believe as everything seems to be going wrong but know this dear reader, God says in *Jeremiah 29:11-14 – 11. For I know the plans I have for you," declares the Lord, "plans to prosper you and not to harm you, plans to give you hope and a future. 12. Then you will call on me and come and pray to me, and I will listen to you. 13. You will seek me and find me when you seek me with all your heart. 14. I will be found by you," declares the Lord, "and will bring you back from captivity. I will gather you from all the nations and places where I have banished you," declares the Lord, "and will bring you back to the place from which I carried you into exile."* Let these scriptures be the foundation of your belief system in the Almighty God and His promises.

- God has a plan and a purpose for all of us. So, amidst our rocky beginnings, mistakes, wilful mis-behaviour called sins, God still loves us and is ready with loving open arms to forgive us as we come to Him with a penitent heart and accept Him, through Jesus Christ, as our Lord and Saviour. He's ready and willing to help us get through and pass our past because He has a promised way, plan and future for us.

Chapter 4

Puppy love & school in town

When I came to Kingston at age four (4) I started attending Waterloo Preparatory School which was operated by the Mennonite Church. As a child, I loved it for the most part, because there were lots of fun things to experience such as slides, merry- go- round, and swings etc. Coming from a rural parish, I was very shy, behaved differently, and talked differently, and to top it all, most of the children weren't as dark-skinned as I am, so it took a while for me to 'thaw out' so to speak, and for them to reach out to me.

I must tell you, when I came from 'country' (this is how we call rural areas in Jamaica), I didn't eat much, and the food tasted different from what I used to eat. I had to acquire the taste for these new foods and how they were prepared. Mi Auntie coulda cook and bake gud! (My Aunt could cook and bake well). She was a ''foodie'' too, but she got me to start eating more over time.

Breaking the Mold

Another challenge for me was that I ate very slowly, so when it was lunch time at school, everyone ate their lunches and then went to play. When they came back from playing, I was still eating, yes you read right. Ms. Dacres, our teacher, would say, "Ok Rosalee put it away." I therefore had to take home some of the food or give it to my new friend, Margaret. After a while Margaret would say her uniforms were bursting as I was feeding her so much. My teacher eventually told my Aunt to give me less food.

I was considered a brilliant student, as I came from 'country', and after a short while I came 1st in the class. My Aunt would boast that I was bright and after a while I recognized that I had become prideful. This 'prideful' demeanour extended to me also being told that I was pretty and dressed in beautiful clothes. Pride isn't a good trait and later in my adult life I had to renounce it.

As I was getting comfortable at Waterloo Preparatory School, (which was really like a Kindergarten-type of school, based on the education system in Jamaica), it was now time for me to move on to the Primary School level. My Aunt organized for me to attend the ''New Day All Age School'', which has a totally different school population size, total size and culture. My Aunt tried to prepare me by telling me that there were no play times or playground rides etc. By now I was six (6) years old, but the dilemma arose, how can a six years (6) old process that kind of information? I was totally crushed and disappointed when I visited the school and didn't see any play area or equipment like my other school grounds, so I dreaded this new school at the outset.

The children were aggressive, begged a lot, and spoke more of the Jamaican creole that I used to hear and even speak a bit of, while I lived in 'the country'. They considered me 'stoosh' in comparison to them because it was said that I spoke with an American accent. I carried lunch to school every day up to grade 6 (even to high school), and I wasn't interested in the popular school diet of patties and coco bread. I was too 'prim and proper' for them, and I didn't like the 'rowdy games' that they all played and seemed to like.

One day two of my classmates decided that they were going to fight me, and I really can't recall why; however, I learnt quickly that it didn't take much for the children to fight with each other. I was very scared as I wasn't an experienced fighter. The only person I tried to fight was Sophia, who didn't usually retaliate. Well, the girls were raining down some blows on me, and I just had to defend myself.

I was instantly reminded of when God asked Moses, in Exodus 4:2, "What do you have in your hand." Well, I realized that I was fearful like Moses, I had no staff in hand except my sturdy '*'Return of the Jedi*'' red metal lunch box. I closed my eyes and swung my weapon and the next moment I heard screams, as my weapon connected with the girls. Still in a state of fear, I barely opened my eyes, and saw that my opponents were nursing wounds. I then took the opportunity of making a hasty retreat across the road (dwl). With much caution, the next day I saw them at school, and they had the nerve to tell me they had ''cocos'' (swellings) on their foreheads and elbows. We made a truce and became friends after that.

As the years progressed, I became more integrated and comfortable in the school, and by about grade 5, I started playing some of the very 'rowdy games' I had shunned in the beginning. I even started to stay behind after school to play a primarily girls' game of 'dandy-shandy', with a ball made from a juice box stuffed with paper. It was such fun.

Aunt Velma instructed me to come home promptly after school unless I was doing extra lessons, and she was very serious, therefore, staying behind was me just being disobedient. Before we moved to a different location that was a bit farther in distance to the school, she would sometimes appear on the road, but not seemingly necessarily coming for us. This would surprise both of us, but I would pretend it didn't affect me.

I remember one such time Sophia and I were going to school on the evening shift. We had walked one part of the way, and as we were climbing some heaps of dirt and having fun, the next thing we felt were licks raining down on us. Yes, you guessed it, Aunt Velma had walked the other way, and caught us getting ourselves dirty and having fun doing so. Oh boy, I got into so many more scrapes because I loved playing and having fun.

I also now recall that when we lived in the Mona area, Aunt Velma would set up her friends and neighbours as 'watchmen' to report our actions to her. To be fair to her, she loved us and wanted to protect her sister's children even when she wasn't around.

Rosalee Kidd-Mighty

Puppy-Love

My "puppy-love" experience started on the first day that I walked into Grade 2. Yes, *'he'* was sitting at a desk, and like two magnets attracting each other, *'he'* turned around and our eyes met. Whew! It was love at first sight in my mind and heart. He was handsome, brown-skinned, brown eyes, and curly hair. I later discovered that his name was Kevin, his mother taught at our school, and his older sister was in the same class as Sophia.

I had the privilege of sitting directly behind him in class, and before long, our love blossomed, or so I thought. One day he told me that another girl in his community liked him, and instantly jealousy took over my eight years old mind and heart. I reacted to the information with anger, promptly telling him, "Don't talk to her!!!." I thought it was as simple as that but learned that life is not so simple after all (laugh). I also had to compete for his affection with 'Janet' in our class, but when he told me it was me that he liked, this was music to my ears.

I was so unashamedly in love that one day I told him to give me his notebook in which I wrote him a message *"telling him"* to put his head under my desk, and I would do the same, so we could kiss. He did put his head under my desk, but I got cold feet and pinched him instead. To my utter surprise and fear, Janet, who was obviously watching us, tried grabbing the book to see what I had written. Kevin alerted me, and threw the book to me, and I was able to hastily erase all trace of our love plans. Whew, that was a close one!!.

During one of our 'talks' Kevin told me that his mother was planning to send him to another school. Disappointed as I was hearing that news, I chose to live in my happy bliss, and told him that it wasn't true, and just continued to enjoy our talks together.

When we started Grade 3, Mrs. Osbourne who was still our teacher, (in fact she was my teacher up to grade 4), would mark the register and as she called Kevin's name, I would blurt out, "Absent miss,". This went on for a while until one day she told me that Kevin was attending another school. What!!, I thought, how could this be?, my poor nine (9) years old heart couldn't take this news. Luckily, I was seated because I suddenly felt very weak, and my heart was 'like' breaking into pieces. Naturally I was very sad for a while, however, I would occasionally see him when he would visit his mom at school, and even though my now fragile little heart would skip a beat, I would pretend that I didn't see him because I was shy and still liked him a lot.

I remember at Graduation. when I was in grade 5, we had to recite excerpts of Psalm 97, and as we were leaving the stage I saw him, my heart started beating fast and I froze, someone had to nudge me for me to get back to reality. From the looks on Mrs. Osbourne's face, she wasn't very happy either (smile).

I still thought fondly of him for years after, and whenever I saw his sisters I would ask about him. When we were both in high school, me attending Holy Childhood High School, and Kevin attending Calabar High School. A friend of mine had a boyfriend who attended Calabar High School, so I enquired about Kevin, and guess what! He knew Kevin, and as we were all in fifth form at that time, and nearing Graduation time, we all decided to meet up on the last day of fifth form.

Unfortunately, though, I wasn't a part of the happy throng going to Hope Botanical Gardens, as my Aunt who was very intuitive, overprotective and strict, told me, "Fine, yuh yaad afta school dun." (Come home right after school ends). She said no to the trip to the Gardens with my '*girlfriends'*, and on reflection, I had wisely not told her that boys were going to attend. Naturally I was very angry, disappointed and sad for a very long time, however, looking back, I concluded that God knows best, he knew what could have happened, and exactly what he was saving me from.

Continuing my journey involving Calabar High School, I remember that Mrs. Osbourne kept in touch with my Aunt about my progress after I graduated from New Day All Age School and started High School. She learnt that I was not doing well in Mathematics, so she graciously paid for me to attend Saturday extra lesson classes, guess where?? Calabar High School!!.

I had a dreadful stint there because I didn't learn much. The primary reasons were: (1) I was terrified of the predominantly male presence (being an all-boys school population) because of my past ordeal with males (2) I was extremely insecure and didn't have much confidence in my abilities; (3) I had a mental block for Mathematics. This 'block' originated while I was at New Day All Age School. In Grade 6 as the Teacher,

Ms. Russell started writing *'M'* for Mathematics class I would break out in profuse sweating. It was so bad that even my hands and feet would sweat. I truly hated the subject, but thankfully I overcame that fear while I was pursuing a university degree. Guess what? I got A's and B's in Algebra and Calculus 1 & 2.

In Grade 5, all students are being prepared to sit a national examination, referred to then as the 'Common Entrance Examination', which sets the qualifying standard for entry into High Schools across the island. Unfortunately, I was not successful in that examination, much to the utter disbelief and disappointment of my Aunt and Mrs. Christie, Vice Principal of New Day All Age School. I was even more disappointed in myself, as, despite the challenge with Mathematics, I knew that I had the ability and knowledge of all the subjects I did, and that I could and should have aced them all. My disappointment in myself was made worse by the jeers being extended to me by other students who saw me as a 'sure pass'.

Fortunately, I had another chance to redo the said examination, so I tried working much harder while in Grade 6. I continued to struggle with Mathematics, even continuing to do extra lessons in the subject. I recall praying to God telling him that I dreaded sitting the up-coming Common Entrance Examination and that I needed his help to be successful. The day of the examination appeared to come even quicker than I realized and expected. As I sat waiting for the Invigilator to give the order to start writing, I had memory block in one of the subjects, but I believe God answered my prayer, as I eventually remembered a little more before the Invigilator said ''put your pencils down''. I knew I did the best that I could, but I was still unsettled in my mind that I had done an excellent job. It didn't help that Aunt Velma was not too confident about my efforts either. When it was announced that the results would soon to be posted in the newspaper, I could neither sleep nor eat for that period, as my stomach was in knots with fear of failing yet again.

Thankfully, I saw my name in the newspaper, I was successful and was placed at my first choice, Holy Childhood High School, an all-girls High School. It was a moment celebration because it was all God's work. I was so grateful and thanked God for helping me to pass.

While at Holy Childhood High School, I performed very well at the outset, but somehow, I became complacent. My reasoning is that the Teachers were not the types to which I had become accustomed, that is, they do not mete out beatings for work not done at high performance levels, and my Aunt wasn't somehow as strict as before. The school had grades ranging from A-G, G being the highest grade for high performing students. When I started out, I was in E stream, but was later demoted to B. The 'slide' was shocking and painful, and only my sister knew. Somehow my Aunt found out, and needless to say she was 'hopping mad'. I was so embarrassed and low in spirit, still doubting myself, and didn't have the willpower to work as hard as I could and should.

While experiencing this low energy feeling, we had to move to another area, and this increased my distress, as I didn't have any friends in this new neighbourhood. I continued in my mediocre work level, sat seven (7) subjects in the general school-leaving examination at the time, and was successful in four (4) subjects. Looking back, I knew I could have done so much better, but I had such self-defeating thoughts, and doubted myself a lot.

After High school, I recall a Deacon at the Church at which I was worshipping at the time, asking me what I wanted to do as a career focus. I told him Journalism. He said I should research all that was required, and he would arrange for the church to assist me. I was excited but dreaded it.

I felt relief when my Aunt allayed my fears when she told me I was going to work now that I had finished High School, just like my sister did. On reflection, I believe that decision was best, for that season, because of my sustained negative and low-energy mindset, which were mostly caused by my doubts about my abilities.

Encouragement #4

- A positive mindset allows you to learn in all situations, so look out for the many lessons in life, and learn from the impact they have over your life. While 'School' is a necessary and formal place of education and knowledge, we can be taught life lessons through experiences, nature, animals, by a beggar, janitor, boss, child, king etc., so be open-minded to learning much from the non-traditional schools and sources, which are characterized in some quarters as being crude and unstructured. The lessons learned can have life-changing impact.

- I remember reading "Gifted Hands" the life story of Dr. Ben Carson (A pioneer in the field of neurosurgery), in which he said that as a medical Doctor, he ensured that he spoke with the Nurses because he learned so much about his patients from them. He didn't spend as much time with the patients as the nurses did, so he learned to trust their observations and suggestions. The key takeaway is to be humble and open minded when the unstructured school is in session.

Chapter 5

The long-term impact of being sexually abused and near-death experiences

When a person is sexually abused, especially at a young age, unless they get psychological help early, they will sometimes act out what has been embedded in their minds and bodies, not conscious that they are doing harm to themselves or others. I am showing you that I understand some of your struggles, and guess what, they are not unique to you. There are so many others who are also suffering in silence, and ashamed of their thoughts and actions.

I am therefore encouraging and empowering you, yes you, to get up and seek help. Do not let your past and your circumstances define who you truly are, and that God loves you even when others don't.

In the neighourhood that we lived at that time, there was a young man, Chinese in ethnicity but also dark-skinned. His name was Paul (he died many years ago). I found that I was attracted to him, and he was also attracted to me, however, I recognized that he wanted to be deeply intimate with me, and I certainly wasn't up for that activity, so the ''attraction'' went immediately. I soon realized that I had normal feelings as any normal woman does, but once these feelings were challenged with any attempts towards engaging in sexual activities, I just freeze up with fear, anger, and other emotions that I can't always describe. It's as if I'm being abused all over again, I didn't trust men and didn't allow them to get too close to me.

I must add though, that there had been times when I would think of ''going rogue'', but instantly the fleeting thought goes away, as I would see my Aunt's face appearing before me. Therefore, I didn't do a lot of things, whether bad or even not so bad, in my view, because of fear of my Aunt's discipline. This plus other things caused me to live a very timid life, and not the purposeful life God called me to live, especially at that time of my life.

On another occasion I recall that as I tried to converse with a young man from next door, 'Sonia' called me and told me to ''be careful so I wouldn't get pregnant while on holidays''. What! I thought, how could just chit chatting with this young man get me pregnant?, he didn't even stimulate me intellectually nor romantically. My immediate response to ''Sonia's'' warning was that she has nothing to be worried about because I knew exactly what and who I wanted for my life, and this young man was not included. I felt bad after that reaction because I knew that she was only expressing concern about me and my safety and welfare.

From I was in my teenage years, I knew within myself that I did not have much tolerance for ''small talk'' that were obviously a ''come-on-to-me'' strategy, especially from young men who did not stimulate me intellectually as well. This attitude made me appear and labeled a ''snob'', but it was one of my safeguards and boundary-setting to prevent me having to fend off potential unwanted sexual attacks, and these happened frequently enough, and in the most overt and disgusting ways at times.

Near-death Experiences

In addition to my sexual abuse and other issues, I recall at least two (2) ''near death experiences, but for the grace of God, who sent his protecting angels to rescue me, because, as I believe it, he wasn't finished with me, my life, and my purpose.

The first experience happened when I was about eight (8) years old. My uncle Basil (Sonia's brother) decided to take the family on a trip to 'Dunn's River Falls', a local tourist attraction venue in Ocho Rios, in the parish of St. Ann. These ''Falls'' are a majestic waterfall flowing into the sea, a breath-taking, refreshing, soothing and resplendent beauty to behold and experience. As we were climbing them and having the greatest fun seeing who could master them to the top, I slipped from a rock and disappeared under the water. In my mind, I was under water far too long, I believed I was dying, and no one was aware or would save me. God allowed Uncle Basil to see it all, and he rescued me from drowning that day. I was so shaken that my tears fell from my eyes just like the water was flowing from the ''Falls'' into the sea.

The second experience took place one day when I was trying to go across a busy and heavy-trafficked highway crossing along Constant Spring Road. Although traffic flowed in one direction only, I remember looking to my right at the oncoming traffic. Seeing none coming at the time, I stepped onto the road ready to cross, when suddenly and seemingly out of nowhere, a blue Volkswagen motor car came barreling down the road directly for me.

I was transfixed, I couldn't scream, move, or even breathe. Suddenly I felt a hand grab me and pull me back on to the sidewalk, and to safety. I was so shocked, I couldn't talk, only bawled uncontrollably. After I calmed down sufficiently to speak, ''my hero angel'' whose name I can't recall being told, enquired of me about my feelings etc. Eventually as he was satisfied that I was fine, he guided me across the road to safety. No one can convince me that this is not the grace and work of God that, yet again, he's showing me that he is not finished with me yet.

Part of my story and journey also included moments when I went through rebellion, and occasionally downright rudeness and malicious behavior. As a result of these behaviours, for which I now know, and understand, are wrong I take responsibility for as I'm a Christian. I created offences and hurt other persons. The tragedy about this is that I didn't feel any remorse then, and on the few occasions that I felt the need to apologize, I did so. Telling lies was also heightened, particularly to get myself out of situations where I could.

Encouragement #5

- As much as possible, be intentional about always speaking the truth. Ultimately, you will be and feel liberated.

Two rules I learnt as a child.....

> *"Speak the truth and speak it ever*
> *Cause it what it will*
> *For he who hides the wrong he did*
> *Does the wrong thing still"*

- Golden Rule: Matthew 7:12 (NIV), "So in everything, do to others what you would have them do to you, for this sums up the Law and the Prophets" "

- Confess your sins to the Lord, seek and accept his forgiveness, and believe Jesus Christ as your Lord and Saviour. Love others as He has loved you by his dying on the Cross to save your life, and to give you eternal life in Him.

Chapter 6

I have decided to follow Jesus....no turning back......

As I shared before, I grew up with Christians all around me, and from an early age I had a vivid consciousness of God and heaven, and what was going on ''up there''. I remember having the belief as a child, that whenever I would hear the thunder rolling, I had this imagery of people in heaven rolling gigantic drums of water thereby causing the deep and heavy sounds. Whenever I saw the flashes of lightning followed by the rain, the imagery and belief were that the lightning was caused by metals rubbing together causing gashes of light, and the rains were water being poured out from the drums.

I recall having a vision at age eight, while standing in the dining room. In the vision, I was seeing myself in the future that I was going to be great, and I would be on television. I shared that vision with Aunt Velma, and she had a hearty laugh at what I told her. I was not fazed by her reaction, and I was convinced that I was seeing something that was going to happen, although I didn't understand how it would happen. (I now know that it was the Holy Spirit of God giving me a revelation of my future).

Fast-forwarding to a few occasions as I got older, I have had the opportunity of being on television in the year 1994, when I was a contestant in the Jamaica Festival Queen competition, and as part of the festival celebrations I was in the Float Parade which was used to showcase the queen and other contestants. This was televised so I experienced my first television appearance. I was in a 'Singer' advertisement, and I also represented Jamaica Promotions Corporation (JAMPRO) as a client service officer in 'The Blackburns', a television series on CVM television. Although these occasions were real, I somehow knew that there was a greater meaning and purpose for these activities in my life, and not just ''to be on television''.

I also had conversations with God, and developed a personal relationship with Him wherein I would ask Him for things and for help to get me out of trouble. I also asked him for protection and told him about the injustices I experienced. He always seemed to grant me my requests, some of which I have already shared in my story, and as I got older, I therefore learned to give Him thanks and praises, throughout my continuing life issues and journey.

However, I didn't make a commitment to accept Jesus Christ as Lord of my life, until I was seventeen (17) years old. At that age and time, acceptance to me meant that I became a believer in the Christian faith and doctrine, and that I was not going to go to hell.

Many times, before accepting Him I would feel the pull of God on my heart, and I would often quench it. At church I would go to the altar a few times but pulled back from total acceptance, with one of my reasons being that I didn't want to start and then return to my life of 'wrong-doings', by my standards. Some examples are; fighting Sophia because I felt like doing it, not cleaning my room as was expected, reading steamy romance novels (Mills & Boon, Harlequin etc.) while pretending that I was studying schoolwork. I was also conscious of the continuing presence of sins in my life, such as lying, pride, malice, jealousy, anger, disobedience, etc., which I knew displeased God.

My second reason was that I thought and believed that I wasn't good and clean enough, having had all those bad experiences in my life, feeling guilty about them, and that I would have to 'clean myself up' before I could accept Jesus Christ as my Lord and Saviour. Bwoy, was I wrong,!!

After reaching home from going to the altar at a crusade, I asked my sister Sophia to tell me how I could become 'good' before I accepted Jesus as my Saviour. She patiently and lovingly explained to me that I can't be good on my own, I had to fully accept Jesus Christ into my heart and life as my Lord and Saviour, believe that He died on the cross to save me from my sins, confess that I am a sinner, repent of my sins and ask for forgiveness. Then, God forgives me, and the Holy Spirit will take up residence in my heart and help me to live the good life he called me to live.

I was relieved, and the very next Sunday I started going to New Members (Believers) class, (a class to learn more about Christianity, knowing and accepting God, and about the church doctrines), and got baptised in November 1991. *Reality check!!* After five (5) months I soon learnt that being a Christian didn't safeguard me from being hurt, from bad things happening to me, and from me sinning, when I was severely tested.

I came to understand during the time of testing as I walked in the faith, that being a Christian meant that I had to surrender my entire life to Jesus Christ, that is, all parts of my mind, body, soul and spirit. I couldn't give Him the parts I wanted Him to have and keep back parts of me. Let's face it, Christianity isn't an easy and problem-free journey, and surrendering to our God is a daily, hourly, minutely, secondly, activity.

The Church fellowship I attended provides someone called a 'Sponsor' who would walk alongside New Christian believers and encourage and support them. I came to realize too that we can put on a façade and reveal what we want to show others while hiding other things. I still had deep dark and dirty secrets that I kept in my heart, there was a contradiction and confusion in my mind and heart as to how to become free so that the Holy Spirit could reside and have freedom to do His work in me. These secrets became my "gods", and took a paramount place in my life, manifesting in fear, worry, doubts, self-defeating thoughts etc.

My situation brought me to reflect on the scripture passage in the Bible from the book of Matthew chapter 6 verse 24 which reads: *(NKJV), "No one can serve two masters; for either he will hate the one and love the other, or else he will be loyal to the one and despise the other. You cannot serve God and mammon.".* 'Mammon' according to the Oxford dictionary is wealth regarded as an evil influence or false object of worship and devotion.

Encouragement #6

- My friend, you can't continue to give all these self-defeating thoughts a paramount place in your heart any longer. It will cause you to be always looking at your past and not what is currently going on in your life. It will also cast doubts on your bright future. Consider this, you are driving your car, and your eyes are constantly fixed on the rear-view mirror and not on the road ahead, what do you think will happen? Yes, you will crash!

- I implore you, look ahead, seek God for yourself now, not later, nor tomorrow or next week. Now! Bawl out to Him, tell Him all your secrets, concerns and struggles. Trust Him, listen to Him, hold on to Him and don't let go, for He already knows what you are facing, and He is ready and able to help you.

- Come take His hand, pray this prayer to Him: ''Lord today I am crying out to you, I am giving all my worries to you, you know them, I can't do this any longer, I don't want to do this any longer. I choose to accept the good, purposeful life you have for me. Lord, I am ready to take the next step according to **Romans 10:9** - I confess with my mouth that Jesus is Lord and believe in my heart that God raised him from the dead''.

- If you prayed this prayer you are saved. Congratulations my friend, I am rejoicing with you as well as Jesus and the angels in heaven!

- Next steps: Purchase a physical Bible or download a Bible app, read it and seek the Holy Spirit for understanding and His help to find a Church near you that believes in Jesus Christ. Tell them you have accepted Jesus Christ as your Lord and Saviour, and you want to be baptised.

- Not because you become a Christian you automatically stop sinning, and all your struggles dissipate. No, it's a process, and as you go through your struggles God is there with you and He will strengthen you. As you rely on Him more you will realize that amidst the hottest battles you can go through only with His divine help.

Chapter 7

Work, the process of being faithful

I started working in the corporate world in November 1991, and was learning loads of stuff that were not printed in a textbook. During this stage, unfortunately, I got somewhat caught up in the culture and environment of the time, and therefore experienced some not-so-good changes in my Christian walk, behaviour, speech, etc.

My first job was at Post and Telecommunications Office (CSO) and I was assigned to the Telecommunications Department. I worked among some people who I found to be nice and pleasant, while others were cold and unkind. Among the ''nice and pleasant'' ones I met Charmaine, and we became friends even to today, in fact, she is regarded as a family friend.

Over the passage of time, there were many other staffers with whom I had pleasant relationships, and who made a strong and positive impact on my life while working in that environment.

I choose to make special mention of one co-worker, Mr. Reitz, a kind, pleasant and caring gentleman, and a Pastor. He encouraged me to do Word Puzzles to improve my knowledge and language skills, and to be a good Christian. He was like a Father to me. It was a very sad and frightening moment when one day while on vacation I received a telephone call from my Aunt Velma, advising me that Mr. Reitz had died. This news was such a great shock and disappointment to me, as for the years I have known him, he was a good friend, Counselor, and a father to me. Work and the workplace were not the same to me and others who had the same view of him as I did,

Along the way during my work life at the company, I had some personal encounters with males which didn't materialize into any long-term relationships, primarily because from early into these associations I discovered that the intentions were always leading towards sexual encounters. I was in no way ready for this type of encounter and had already decided that it would not happen until and unless I was married. In other cases, I just did not yet find ''the one'' with whom I was compatible, moreso that I am a Christian who wanted to serve God in spirit and in truth.

In 1996, however, I started working at a Life Insurance Company, where I met Sophia Richards, and with whom my Christian walk intensified. Sophia was bold, talkative and passionate for Christ. My desire was always for more of God, but I didn't know how to move forward. Yes, I attended church, was active in the dance and drama ministries but there was an emptiness that was gnawing at me.

One day I was talking to another Christian lady at work about my desire, and she simply said, "Just tell God that you want more of Him and you want to hunger and thirst after Him." Wow, I thought, as simple as that eh!!, It was like a weight had lifted off me, so I began praying that way. Did things change immediately, not at all as I still struggled with my fears, doubts, and insecurity.

However, with my ''mustard seed'' level of faith, I knew God listened and that he is ''a rewarder of those who diligently seek Him''. So, the process of being more patient and faithful had started. The book of Hebrews 11:6 sums it up beautifully: *''But without faith it is impossible to please Him, for he who comes to God must believe that He is, and that He is a rewarder of those who diligently seek Him''.*

One of my dreams was always to work with an airline, and I got that chance in 1998. Yeah!!! I had applied for such a job and was successful with a position at the then Air Jamaica (Jamaica's National airline).

I had some serious challenges at work. Unfortunately, my insecurity, fear, and the strong work culture and demands had made me very uncomfortable, and it reached the stage where I would literally cry each morning because I didn't want to go to work.

I was slow in doing my work and made too many mistakes. This made me a conversation piece in the office, but thanks be to God for some powerful prayer partners and support system I had at church, I was able to be strengthened and persevered for a while. My situation became even more intense, and one day upon hearing my Supervisor say: "I am going upstairs", I had an overwhelming feeling of doom. I heard the Holy Spirit say to my spirit, "you will soon get a call from upstairs."

Let me back track a bit, when I was being introduced to the staff and they reached this Supervisor, the hairs on my body literally stood on ends and I heard, not audibly, but in my spirit, "Be careful of this woman." Wow, I was in shock I don't think I remember the Lord speaking to me like that before.

So, back to the impending call....I started praying frantically for the Lord's intervention. I did get the call about 5 minutes afterwards from the Director of Administration, who invited me to come up to her office. I used this time to continue praying, "God don't let me cry in front of these people, give me boldness to speak and if I am going to be asked to leave let it not be at this time."

Whoa! I went to the office, and it was like I was in a court room but a smaller version. I sensed that my 'advocate' though invisible was very present, this is my assurance that my God said he would never leave me nor forsake me.

My Supervisor, the Administrative Supervisor and the Director were there in the room. I sat quietly and listened as the list of my faults were rolled out: I made a lot of mistakes, I was slow, I was anti-social etc.

When it was my turn to speak, I said, "I have heard all the negatives, what are the positives?" The Director stared me straight in my eyes and said she had not heard of any. This hit me to the core of my being, and I could feel myself crumpling to the ground on the inside. I was shocked, the Administrative Supervisor tried to give me tips on improvement, but nothing was penetrating my crushed heart. As a result of this assessment, my Probationary period was extended by three (3) months. I was totally humiliated as other staff were asking after a time why I wasn't yet wearing uniform. Some knew already but asked as a sham. Eventually I was placed on staff, but my trepidation remained.

When I pondered on all that happened, I thought it very strange that the organization would allow a staff member who wasn't performing well on the job to remain as an employee, but I gave all credit, glory and honor to God for his love, grace and mercy in my circumstances. Again, he showed me how faithful he is, and how true His promises are. This situation propelled me to pray even harder, and to treasure the prayerful support of my friends with their constant prayers. It was also very encouraging when I overheard two staff members talking about how well I was working. Prayers do change things for the better.

Breaking the Mold

Despite these positives, I still really didn't think I was doing a good job, until one day the Senior Director rushed through the office door and started looking around. I was very frightened and almost fell from my chair when he asked, "Who is Rosalee Kidd-Mighty?" I thought I was going to die, my heart was beating very fast, my mouth was dry, my eyes seemingly about to pop right out of the sockets, my knees were weak and shaky, and a million negative thoughts flashed into my mind all at the same time. What did I do now, I pondered?

I made a weak raise of my hand as I didn't trust my voice, and he strode powerfully over to me with outstretched hand. He said loudly, "I had to come personally down here to shake your hand and tell you that you are doing a fantastic job!" "What!" I screamed inside, "me"?, what was he saying!!, ''me" who didn't believe I was doing a good job?"

I was teary-eyed and speechless, and I barely whispered my thanks as he went on to tell me what I had done. This is just like God; because of how he knew I was seeing myself, He got the 'big man upstairs' to come down to commend me on a job well done.

I worked in the Purchasing Department, which is responsible for purchasing all items the airline needed, let's just say from a pen to an aircraft part. We were also responsible for all the repairs of airline equipment, machinery etc., so, just like your car, after a period you must service, and so it is with the aircraft. The repairs and troubleshooting are called 'checks', and the aircrafts are sent back to their manufacturers for these 'checks'.

One (1) of my roles was to ensure that all the aircraft parts for the 'checks' that needed repairs, were sent overseas to different repair companies to be repaired and are transported in time to the manufacturers who were doing the' checks'. I also had to negotiate payment plans and/or arrange payments with the repair companies and our payables department. Even though I got a short turn-around time in which to organize everything, all the parts were released and received in time for the 'check'. That was what the Senior Director commended me for.

In looking back, all I can say is God is good, and this verse of scripture comes to mind: Galatians 6:9 Amplified Bible, Classic Edition

" And let us not lose heart and grow weary and faint in acting nobly and doing right, for in due time and at the appointed season we shall reap, if we do not loosen and relax our courage and faint".

In the year 2003, the entire department, excluding the Manager and her Secretary, were made redundant. I was a bit prepared for the announcement because I was alerted of the information a few minutes before.... All staff were called to a meeting at which the announcement of redundancy was made. For some unknown reason, at the time, I was not as perturbed as I thought I would have been, and after the announcement was made, I was at peace in my spirit and looked forward to receiving my redundancy payment and a travel package. Most other persons were crying and couldn't understand why I wasn't. The reason for my "peace" was that some time before the redundancy took place, I had enquired of the Lord about leaving the job. He had told me that "my work" there wasn't finished, but on the day of the redundancy I knew "my work" was finished. God's work for me at Air Jamaica was finished and eventually two (2) of my friends, Marcia and Neil, accepted Jesus Christ as Lord and Saviour of their lives, all glory to God.

I was unemployed for three (3) months but went to several interviews each week. By God's divine grace and providence, one of my church Sisters was the Human Resource Manager at Jamaica Promotions Corporation (JAMPRO), and I told her I was seeking a job. She took my resume and told me that she couldn't just give me a job but will inform me of any suitable vacancies so I could apply and be subjected to being interviewed. Well, I went on two (2) interviews and was chosen for the last one to be the Administrative Assistant for the Business Development & Communications Departments. This happened in 1994. While I was grateful for the job, the Administrative Assistant position required me to do tasks that I frankly didn't like, such as filing, taking notes and preparing minutes, which ironically constituted most of my job functions.

I consider myself to be a Pioneer, in the sense that I would always be able to come up with new ideas and find creative and easier ways of doing things. I was passionate about serving, but one of my negative traits is that I quickly got bored, impatient and frustrated with doing the same things repeatedly. I felt guilty for procrastinating, and not doing my best at times when I saw the undone minutes and papers for filing, and the more the delays the more I felt overwhelmed. I had no one to blame but myself, and I marveled that I still got good evaluations.

My boss, Lisa Bell, was a truly remarkable person and an excellent boss. When she was promoted to Executive Director of the Business Development Division, I was also promoted to the position of Executive Assistant possibly because I also excelled in other areas like communication, customer service, planning and executing events.

When a position for Client Service Officer became available, I jumped at the opportunity, and I excelled in this position. The position entailed me being one of the first points of contact for the organization, as well as providing exporters with pertinent information for export etc. I got special commendations from clients, the President, other staff, and from a 'Mystery Shopper' survey. As a result of the latter, in 2014 I was asked to represent the Company, and Jamaica, on a business study tour in Nicaragua, where we looked at best practices for Latin and Caribbean Trade Promotion Agencies. As part of the deliverables from the study tour, I created and presented ideas to improve our Trade Promotion Agency.

All the places that I had worked I volunteered and organized social events to build camaraderie. This place of employment was no different and I was a member of the Staff Association and served in numerous roles. Additionally, I was one of the founding members of 'Services Flex', an entity created to build camaraderie, improve staff morale and plan events.

As I've decided to be brutally honest about my experiences and my faults throughout my story, I admit that I was a ''complainer'' and with a bad attitude, as well as a 'faultfinder'. I not only complained too much at times, but was also critical about new initiatives which I deemed senseless. Even when my points of view were reasonable, sadly, my reactions were sometimes pride-filled and immature.

The Holy Spirit convicted me about this unchristian-like behavior, and I was made to see the negative impact my behaviour was having on my coworkers; so, when my new manager was going through my evaluation with me, she told me clearly and firmly among other things that I behaved too emotional at times. In fact, she was spot-on with some of the very things the Holy Spirit convicted me about.

She was pleasantly surprised at my ready acknowledgement, and that I sat humbly before her, receptive of the feedback, and agreed with her. I apologized to her and did my stint of repentance with the Holy Spirit. After that session, and with the Holy Spirit's help I made a 180 degrees turn around. At my next evaluation, my manager commended me and said she was beginning to wonder if I was the manager or her.

With my new attitude I took new staff under my wings and taught them. I felt good but amidst all the commendations and me even being President for one day, yes, you read right (It was an initiative to build staff morale and my name was pulled in the raffle.) I felt like I was suffocating, and I kept on crying out to God that I wanted to leave the job.

My passion for staff welfare and the betterment of my nation had me starting numerous prayer initiatives with staff and even with other friends who were employed at other Government agencies.

One day in the year 2014 during my conversations with God, through the Holy Spirit, he prompted me to start looking at resignation letters, which I did, then He told me to write my resignation letter with an effective date which he also gave me. I must admit that I wrote the letter but wanted to make sure that it was indeed the prompt of the Lord, and not my own mind. I put the question directly to the Lord: "Is that you Lord, I am not sure if it is you talking". I felt a measure of peace in my spirit about leaving the job at that time, so I did what he told me and presented the letter, even though I didn't know where I was going next.

Simply, I had stepped out in faith, and I knew without a doubt that my time there had ended. At the farewell party the company held on my behalf, I listened keenly as staff at various levels commended me for my excellent work ethics. The Tributes and comments were very nice, but the ones that made me really excited were those which were spoken about how I reflected Christ, and how I encouraged those persons. I was satisfied that I had done God's will during my tenure, so I was pleased, and He received his glory. Sometime after I left the company another staff member informed me that she had recently given her heart and life to the Lord Jesus Christ. God be praised!!! Amen!!

Encouragement #7

- Be careful of whom you listen to, not everyone has your best interest at heart, and some may mean well towards you, but their advice is not always filled with wisdom.
- Be kind to other persons even if or when they are not kind to you ..... *"therefore, whatever you want men to do to you, do also to them, for this is the Law and the Prophets"*.

- Remember that whatever you sow you will definitely reap many times more. *Galatians 6:7, "Do not be deceived: God is not mocked, for whatever one sows, that will he also reap."*; therefore, if you are unkind or unloving to others the same will be meted out to you. On the other hand, if you are kind and loving to others you will receive the same from others.

Chapter 8

Anticlimax - my 18th birthday!

As previously mentioned, after I was baptized, I started my first job in November 1991. I was excited because I would be 18 in a few months. I shared with Aunt Velma and Aunt Pearl that when I turned 18, I could vote, live on my own and even get married. I was truly looking forward to turning 18.

One day, Aunt Velma told Sophia and I that a handsome young man would soon be living next door. We looked at each other and smiled because we knew when she said handsome that's the farthest thing from the truth. Well, make no mistake, Aunt Velma was 'spot-on this time. In my eyes He was very gorgeous but did not have the height that I prefer. Nevertheless, my interest instantly peaked.

Initially, he was very aloof, but gradually we started talking with each other, sharing personal information about age and some background history. He was two years older than I was, had a girlfriend, and a baby girl. My guard went up, but I still had an interest in knowing more about him and engaging him in conversation.

Soon, my friend Charmaine, *John (changed his name) and I, had become fast friends. We girls didn't care much for his girlfriend whom we eventually saw and assessed in a negative light. After a while though, we came to soften towards her realizing that her aloofness may be due to her challenges of dealing with a teenage pregnancy and having and caring for a young child. We accepted that we could have been in the same situation, but for the grace of God, and I then realized that we should never pass judgement on anyone until and unless we too have gone through the same experiences as they have.

I was emotionally and physically attracted to this young man, yet one thing that was lacking was that he did not believe in God, so the spiritual element was a challenge. Lack of wisdom, and my flesh rising, didn't stop me from pursuing my feelings of attraction, despite the warning I got from my Aunt to stay away from him. I was also encouraged by the information Charmaine gave me that he said he found me "sexy" but I was too young. He started showing me lots of attention and I felt so pleased at the prospect of still maintaining contact with him.

One Saturday he told me that he wanted me to come to his workplace and we would be alone. Charmaine advised and cautioned me against accepting this invitation, and I was really torn between going and not going. Nevertheless, I didn't go because it would have also meant lying to Aunt Velma, the consequences of which were not appealing to me.

I thought I had escaped that kind of temptation, but early one Friday night *John and I were together just talking, and he started giving me some ''looks'' that were clear signals that he wanted to get intimate with me. Honestly, I too was being affected by the ''looks'', and with Aunt Velma not being at home for the weekend, and Sophia being sound asleep, I was tempted to "throw caution to the wind" and enjoy the moment. For a while my feelings got the better of me, and activities were heightening when alarm bells went off in my head that I should stop things right then. However, he was not letting up so I started to panic and decided this must stop here. I was in the process of raising my hand to push him off, and there Sophia appeared in the doorway, saw us, and went to another room. I nearly died with shock and embarrassment. My heart was pounding so very hard, and a million things bombarded my mind.

*John wanted to continue the activities in his bedroom, but everything was locked down and turned off for me, and only feelings of shame and guilt, and anticipation of Aunt Velma finding out occupied my thoughts. Sleep for the night was absent for me. The next day came, and I couldn't look at *John nor my sister. She didn't say anything to me about what she saw the night before but advised me that she was going to spend the night at one of her friends, for which I was relieved. Foolishly I thought, "when she returns, I can proudly say nothing happened between *John and I while you were

Breaking the Mold

away." My sister left for the day, and I ensured that I stayed inside the house, thus avoiding *John.

He surfaced when Charmaine came over to visit, and we chatted a bit, but I was terrified about what could happen when Charmaine left for her home. I wanted to ask her to stay the night so badly, but I was truly afraid, afraid even to tell her about what happened the night before. I was certainly not my normal chirpy self, and she eventually decided to say goodbye. *John offered to accompany her to the bus stop, and I said good night, but they were surprised that I did not want to go with them. They persuaded me to come along, and I relented.

As I walked to the bus stop I recalled a verse of scripture from the Bible - Psalm 23:4 to be exact, which reads: *"Even though I walk through the valley of the shadow of death, I will fear no evil, for you are with me; your rod and your staff, they comfort me."* However, I did have fear of the evil that I imagined would come, I feared that I would lose my virginity, I didn't feel the presence and comfort of God, and I didn't know what to say or do. I felt all alone. Charmaine noticed my quiet and sad demeanour and enquired if I was feeling okay. My response was that I was having a headache.

The next set of information about my ordeal will be graphic, as I believe that readers who can't relate to my experience should be made aware of how ''the victims'' feel and think during their ordeal, and how ''the villans'' disassociate their minds, thoughts, and actions from their victims.

*John was very chatty as we walked home, and as we reached my house I quickly got in, locked the front and back doors, and even placed a piece of furniture behind the back door. I was....truly..... terrified! Then, I heard a knock on the door, it was *John calling my name. I told him I had gone to bed, but he asked me to open the door. Like a naïve zombie at 17 years old, 18 in 4 days, I got up, and as I opened the door ever so slightly, he pushed pass me saying he just wanted to watch a little TV. I turned on the TV but sat far away from him. However, he eventually came closer and closer to me and re-started his sexually charged activities like from the previous night. Because of my non-responses, he asked me: "How come you were so hot last night and yuh suh cold now?" I told him I didn't want to continue, and tried to push him off, but he was able to overpower me and dragged me into my bedroom. There he forcibly continued his advances despite my tears and pleas for him to stop. Honestly, I was so weakened and afraid that there was no more energy to push him from and off my body. This was like de'ja vu because here again I just can't seem to have the strength to defend myself when I'm attacked like this.

I was crying and felt almost dead on my inside, only my physical body was there, and I heard myself saying, "Oh God.", which *John thought meant that I was enjoying myself as he tore into my body. In that moment I was very upset with God, asking him: "Where are you?", ''why haven't you come to my rescue?''. *John finished his dastardly act, and even tried to cuddle me, but I pushed him away at which he told me that ''next time it won't be so hot''. He then asked me if I wanted him to leave, to which I nodded as yes, and he left.

After *John left, I searched the mattress for blood since I heard that virgins bleed at their first sexual encounter, but I saw no blood. I was confused but quickly hobbled to close and put a baracade at the door. I cried and cried, but strangely, no tears were falling. I was very deeply troubled and felt so empty. How could I face anyone after this assault, who would believe me that I didn't' give my consent, not my Aunt nor my sister, what a predicament!! What if I became pregnant? Suppose I caught a disease? More questions than answers in the moment, and I just wanted to die. How did God say he wouldn't leave me nor forsake me, and here I was torn and hurting? Why didn't He stop it? He was nowhere around, or so I thought. I felt betrayed and couldn't be consoled. I hated *John, I really had liked and trusted him. Infatuation had quickly turned to raw hate. I hated Rosalee too, why didn't she have the strength to scream, fight, and defend herself?

I had very little sleep that night. I awoke the next morning and went to shower, once again my tortured private part was hurting. As I gingerly tried to wash my feminine patch the blood that never came started to flow and mixed with my tears and the water from the shower. This water couldn't wash away my guilt, shame, blame, hurt, regret, disappointment and hatred. ONLY JESUS COULD DO THAT!!! I felt so alone.

A little later 'he' had the audacity to come knocking on my door and asked if I was okay. The look of hatred in my heart that showed on my face met him, and he made a hasty retreat. I was depressed, deeply wounded and extremely worried. My sister came back later that day, and I just couldn't bring myself to tell her. I was in a daze, and I feared that she would blame me because of what she had seen that night. Aunt Velma also returned, and I just kept to myself.

A few days later Charmaine noticed how withdrawn I had become, and she coaxed me to talk, then I told her about the sordid ordeal. She took me to the doctor, and of course they wanted to know if I wanted to press charges. I decided against that course of action, tempting as it was for me to seek to get justice. I didn't have the strength nor the confidence to go through the legal proceedings even though I wanted him to pay. I still wanted to keep it a secret from everyone else.

My birthday, April 15th came but I had no joy, and though I tried hard to put on a facade of happiness, my body and heart ached. On Saturday April 18th there was a Church sports day event, and I really didn't want to go but Charmaine encouraged me to go, and I did. My fears about pregnancy were allayed as my monthly cycle prevailed, thanks be to God!!, but my entire mood and mindset were unchanged. After a period Charmaine eventually told Sophia about my ordeal, and she felt guilty about leaving me alone. She confronted *John, and he said we had both consented and enjoyed ourselves!!!

Over the next month, with no easing up of my depression and state of mind, I allowed myself to conclude that God created me to be sexually abused so I took matters into my own hands and sought revenge on *John, with the help of a friend.

We played a prank on *John and his girlfriend, at her workplace, but it backfired on me. How? She came to my house and confronted me and another of my girlfriends, in the presence and hearing of my Aunt and the landlady, accusing one or both of us of having sexual relations with her boyfriend. I was mortified, this could not be happening; I was weak and sick to the stomach. It got worse because my Aunt and the landlady both asked us if it was true to which, of course, I instantly denied. My friend, who wasn't aware of my ordeal, was so upset that she cursed out John's girlfriend. She did such a good job of defending me, and herself, that eventually there was calm. However, my feelings of shame and guilt were certainly not calmed. There endeth my sojourn with *John!!!.

The process of healing has taken years and years through much repentance, prayer, deliverance, counseling, sharing my story with boldness and without shame or guilt, helping others who have been hurt as badly as, or worse than I have been. I sought solace, healing, strengthening and comfort in God, who makes all things right and possible, and the memories less painful.

I have made my peace with God knowing that he understood all my moments the entire time, even those in which I blamed him for not being there when I needed him to help me. I have also forgiven my abusers, accusers, doubters, and haters, as their involvement and actions were all used by God, as part of his refinement, preparation and purpose for my life. The journey continues for me, at another level, with me being older, wiser, and more spiritually, mentally, and emotionally mature.

Encouragement #8

- All that glitters is not gold...... the attractive external appearance of someone or something is not a reliable indication of their/it's true nature and worth.

- You should never pass judgement on anyone until and unless you too have gone through the same experiences as they have.

- Strive to release yourself, mind, spirit and body, and your issues, into the safe arms of God, through Jesus Christ. Further, seek to forgive and release those persons who knowingly and unknowingly cause you hurt, distress, pain and sorrow, and pray ''for them'' to join with you as children of the kingdom of God.

- Vengeance is the Lord's to take, not you!! It may seem like the "right thing" to do in the moment, but it will always fail because it is done from evil, malicious, and deadly motives. You will be the one who eventually loses. *Romans 12:19 (NLT): ''Dear friends, never take revenge. Leave that to the righteous anger of God. For the Scriptures says, "I will take revenge; I will pay them back" says the LORD.*

- Recognize the truth from the saying: ''Hurting people hurt other people'', whether consciously or unconsciously done at times.

- Even though my dream of being married as a virgin was shattered and, in an instant, I was thrust from childhood into womanhood, I know God is using and has used this mishap to thrust me into my purpose.......My purpose of sharing my story, encouraging and sharpening you, yes you.

- Now as I look at my daughter, instinctively I want to put her in bubble wraps and safeguard her from being hurt, but I can't, I am not God. I teach her, and protect her as much as I can, but I must leave the rest to God. Is this easy? No, I must release her daily into His loving arms. You must do the same and release yourself and your loved ones into His loving arms.

Chapter 9

The devil is a liar....now I am married

My journey to getting married starts here…

My Sunday School Teacher, Miss Marion Blake asked the class: Which one of you plan to get married? I immediately blurted out with a serious and confident facial expression: "Miss, I am not going to get married".

Miss Blake asks me: "Why is that so Rosalee?" "My response was: ''Marriage is crosses, and it isn't going to work!" mimicking the belief of my family and their experiences of which I am aware. "Why do you think so," she enquired. "Miss, hardly anybody in my family is married, and those who are married the marriage isn't going well," I retorted. She replied, "Rosalee, not because those marriages didn't work mean yours isn't going to work."

I shrugged my shoulder, still not convinced. But she was very right.....

There were also other reasons why I personally didn't want to get married. I was downright scared, I hated and was afraid of the sexual part of marriage because....it's painful for me. Further, how could anyone love and marry me after I shared that I was 'soiled'? This was the lie the devil fed me, and I ate that fruit. However, I soon came to realize that God's plan for my future in that direction was still intact. Here goes......

When I was promoted to an older-aged Sunday school class I saw a young man who was already in the class, and my first thought was that he was much older than the rest of us. I got to love this Sunday school class because we were like a family, and we were always going on trips, the kind of fun time that I liked. When the time came for the next set of students to move up to this class age level, the Church had to extend the level for this class as no one wanted to leave. Our Teachers, Sharon and Algie were terrific, and we all felt so comfortable with them. However, I didn't feel comfortable enough to share my dark secrets.

On one of the trips, a friend had taken a photograph of me in my bathing suit, and one day as another friend and I were in the class looking at that photo, the previously mentioned young man decided to peek at it, and I quickly grabbed the photo from my friend. Why did I pull it away? I didn't like the fact that I was in a bathing suit and being looked at by any guy. Ironically, I was later to find out that 'my husband' (details to come) told me that he had liked the said photo.

Another trip was being planned for our class and I volunteered to be the event planner. One of my tasks was to organize the transportation, so I asked the class if anyone knew someone with a bus that we could charter. The same young man who was peeking at my photo said he knew someone, so Sharon, one of the teachers previously mentioned, asked the young man and I to exchange numbers, and organize the bus. Little did I know that this interchange was a precursor for us exchanging vows. My attempts to connect with the young man for an entire week was frustrating and futile, as several messages from me were unanswered, and those were not the days when cellular phones were in operation.

On the Sunday following, as I was sharing my frustration with one of my friends, the young man appeared. I had by this time found out that his name was Doyle. I was very upset, so I did not hesitate to make my mood very visible to him. He acknowledged my friend and I, but I didn't respond, so he came around to face me. He apologized and said the reason he didn't contact me was that he worked on different shifts, and when he got home, he felt that it would have been too late to call me. He also said he didn't get through with the bus. "Okay, thanks," I said grudgingly, and pouted. I must confess that I respected his sensitivity about my feelings, although I didn't let him know.

Our relationship became less tense after that, and we were in the Youth Fellowship (Young Adult program) ministry together on Fridays. At these meetings the group would pray, have devotion, sing and talk about God and topical issues. He would offer me a ride home on a few occasions, and I would accept them. On one occasion he invited me to a cultural event.

It was ironic, but divine, that the over-protective Aunt Velma liked Doyle, so she was quite receptive to me going out with him when invited to do so. I had even reached the stage where I didn't ask her permission to go out with him, I would just tell her that I'm going out with Doyle, although she didn't hesitate to interrogate me about the details of our dates before we left the house. Looking back, I am glad that she had that approach, as she had the Spirit of Discernment, and she would have discerned if a prospective date wasn't the right one for me.

Doyle and I finally got to go out on the cultural event date, and when he picked me up, we were very awkward with each other. I tried to have a good time, but I was nervous as he was. We walked around looking at the various products, and he purchased food and a silver bracelet decorated with fish for me. I was very surprised, and liked the bracelet very much because to me, the fish has a spiritual (Christian) significance.

We started talking more and went out on more dates. My ride home after Youth Fellowship meetings were also secure. Doyle stimulated me intellectually, and gradually emotionally, but there was one draw-back, he wasn't a born-again believer/Christian, so the spiritual stimulation was not there. I had become very wary of having any kind of serious relationship with a non-Christian. Although we continued dating and Aunt Velma liked him enough to entertain him on visits, there was no formal communication that we were ''going steady''. Additionally, once or twice I had reason to question certain of his behaviours, where they caused me to form certain opinions that increased my caution about being serious with him. For example, there was the occasion when he came to my home with 'Fast Food' and he sat in front of me, ate it all and didn't even ask me if I wanted any. I was stunned and angry, and instantly thought he was "a meanie" I didn't say anything to him at the time, but one day I confronted him and he apologized, explaining that he was very hungry, and since I was home, he assumed that I had already eaten my usual lovely home-cooked meal and not wanting to eat a 'fast-food' meal. "You should have still asked me" I said, and he agreed.

I continued to be uncomfortable with him not being a born-again Christian, so I kept praying to God, seeking confirmation whether I was safe in going forward with a relationship with Doyle. I still had some trust issues, so I just didn't want to trust myself to be naïve again, only to be hurt and disappointed. Admittedly, I was still not quite over the treatment with his fast food. I didn't get a direct answer or peace in my spirit, so I decided that the very next time I saw him I would tell him that what we have was over for me.

I didn't see Doyle for a while and quite unexpectedly, one day my sister Sophia asked me: "When last yu hear from Doyle?" My guard instantly went up with the way in which she asked me the question, and somehow, I knew something was amiss. "W...h...aaaa...tttt happen to Doyle?" I stammered impatiently.

She told me he had called to say that he and his sister were in a terrible car accident, she was in the hospital, and the car was written off.

I was shocked at the news, and embarrassed for myself, that here I was rehearsing how I was going to tell him to take a hike, and he and his sister were hurt. I immediately put aside my own thoughts and agenda, prayed for him and his sister, kept in constant touch with them, and allowed the Lord to work on his soul towards salvation. Soon after, glory to God, Doyle accepted Christ as his Saviour.

I got to see a completely new and encouraging side of Doyle, as he took care of his sister, who was in high school at the time. He displayed such maturity, love, care, thoughtfulness and responsibility during his caregiving. He has a quiet disposition, and showed kindness in so many ways, not the "meanie" I thought from one incident. As I said before, a man had to stimulate me spiritually, intellectually, emotionally and physically, and by this time Doyle had fulfilled all those characteristics. I fell in love!!

Our relationship continued to blossom to greater levels, as Doyle was fulfilling a lot of my dreams, including me visiting and exploring new places. We visited each other's families, and I went to places as a part of his family on some of their trips. The "love" was mutual between us, and we had such fun just being in each other's company. There were instances when Doyle would make statements that were suggestive in one sense, yet like declarations towards us being together as in married, for example......

One day I went to Cranbrook Flower Farm in St. Ann with his family, and we took lots of pictures and enjoyed ourselves immensely.

After, Doyle showed me the pictures and I asked him to make copies so I could get a set. His response was, "Rosalee after a while we will only need one set" I shook my head in agreement because I thought I understood but I really didn't.
What Doyle meant, which I soon found out was after we were married, we wouldn't need two sets of pictures. Did you get that understanding? Good for you, I didn't. Well, he didn't propose to me, he just talked it into being like what I just shared and statements like when we are married, we can do 'this' or 'that'.

I was careful not to weigh in too heavily on these statements, but pondered them in my heart, waiting for the day when they would or would not become a reality. On a few occasions I would pointedly speak about the suggestive statements, and he would just smile and become affectionate.

We had our first major disagreement, which also presented a serious challenge to the future of our relationship. Since, I was always seeking more of God, I would attend Christian events and visit other churches to learn more. One night my friend Sophia and some other friends and I decided to attend a prayer meeting at another Church. I invited Doyle and we traveled together after Youth Fellowship Meeting. As the prayer meeting proceeded, some persons started ''speaking in unknown tongues'', and some of those who went up for prayers were "slain in the Spirit".

As I was worshipping God, I felt a nudge, and it was Doyle saying: "I am leaving" and proceeding to go through the door. I told my friends I would soon be back and went after him. I caught up with him in the parking lot and enquired: "Are you okay? He said: "No, I don't feel comfortable with what was happening inside, so I am leaving". I was slow in understanding at first that the leaving wasn't just him going home but....... The interchange between us went like this:

ME: "Okay, I can understand that you are uncomfortable and want to leave, but you took me here and you are going to take me home!" I said angrily.

HIM: "Okay, okay you can go back inside and when you are ready, I will take you home." he said.

By now, in dismay and hot-headedness, I thought: ''You had better know that you're not leaving me stranded here''. I returned to the meeting, but I was so angry that I couldn't worship as I was thinking about our disagreement and didn't feel comfortable having him waiting outside. Soon after, I told my friends I was leaving.

It was a very tense and uncomfortable ride to my home, as this was our first major disagreement. When we reached my home, Doyle accompanied me inside and said he wanted to talk to me. He repeated that he wasn't sure about what was going on in the prayer meeting, and that he could foresee us being married and me taking our children to this type of meeting with which he is uncomfortable. He therefore thinks it would be best if we parted company.

I was shocked but listened quietly and eventually said: "You know that if there is a choice between you and God, do you know who is going to be left behind?, and it is not God"!!! He said goodbye, went through the door, then through the gate and into his car without even turning to look at me. I felt a stab in my stomach, but quickly put up my protective walls. Oh, very well I thought, and I prepared for bed and slept like a baby. You must be wondering, how could I take it like that? The full impact hadn't hit me yet.

It was a few days afterwards that I told my sister and my friend Sophia. They were shocked and asked why I didn't tell them before, if he hadn't called, and if I wasn't going to call him? I told them quite resolutely that I wasn't going to call him because as I had thought about it, I didn't do anything wrong, and Doyle didn't even try to discuss his concern with me, rather, he decided on his own to end our relationship.

I went to Youth Fellowship Meeting about two (2) weeks after that, and Doyle was there. He said hello, I responded in a like manner, but ignored him afterwards. When the meeting ended, I promptly headed through the door, then the gate, and was heading to the bus stop when Doyle met me at the entrance of the church gate in his car. "Where are you going?" he asked. Didn't you know I was going to give you a ride?"

"Give me a ride," I threw back, "I can't expect that from you anymore as we are no longer together." He beckoned for me to get in the car, and I did. As we travelled, he tried to make small talk, but I was not responding. As I was leaving the car, he asked me if he could come inside because he wanted to talk to me. I shrugged my shoulders and said yes.

He sat down nervously and basically told me that his Aunt Clair told him that he was acting foolishly, and he should be happy he had a woman who wanted more of God. I sat quietly, listened and pondered on what he shared.

"So, what do you think?" he asked. I responded: "I didn't like how you dealt with the situation, you didn't even discuss it with me before you decided to end our relationship. Suppose we were married?" He apologized and jokingly said he didn't need a lecture because he already had a mother. We discussed our way forward and decided that we needed to learn more about what happened at the prayer meeting.

We decided to ask for help and assistance from the Slacks who had been two (2) keynote speakers at one of our Youth Fellowship Retreat. Looking back, I can clearly see God's hand in this divine set up, because Doyle and I were the ones who had taken them back to Kingston after the Retreat. After they prayed about our request for assistance, they announced to us, "Yes, we will counsel you for marriage"!! Huh, Doyle and I stared at each other, as we didn't recall making such a request.

We reminded them about what we had asked them for, and they said yes, but that they would also give us pre-martial counselling. We were blown away and agreed that this must be God's work. They counseled us for one year, yes, one full year, before our wedding.

When our Associate Pastor Michael Shim-Hue started counselling us six months prior to our wedding he marveled at our preparedness. We gained a wealth of knowledge from the Slacks about the roles and perspectives of husband and wife in the marriage relationship, and we were taught individually and together. Again, Look at our God!!!

Being the gentleman that he is, Doyle asked Aunt Velma and dada for my hand in marriage. We prayed and decided on November 18, 2000, as our wedding date. Yes, wedding plans were in full swing, and we saw how God worked out things every step of the way. I was working at Air Jamaica at that time and had the privilege of travelling at a reduced rate, as well as for specified family and friends. Doyle and I were able to visit some of his relatives in Fort Lauderdale. We also purchased some of our wedding items, including my ring.

Sophia and I were watching television one day and saw an advertisement that David's Bridal was having their annual sale. We contacted our friends, the Foremans in Miami for accommodation and we made our travel arrangements for that same weekend. When we visited David's Bridal, I was getting frustrated initially as I couldn't find the ideal dress within my budget. One of my friends suggested a dress and I looked at it skeptically, for I didn't think it would suit me. They insisted and I reluctantly tried it on, instantly, the clouds of sadness were replaced with sunshine and smiles as I waltzed out of the store with my perfect bridal dress.

According to plans, our wedding would take place in the parish of St. Ann because Doyle's family lived in that parish, and my family lived in the adjoining parish, St. Mary. The Church service was set for Ocho Rios Baptist Church, and the wedding reception would be at the Hibiscus Lodge, Almond Tree Villa, St. Ann.

I was excited about getting married, and the wedding, but unfortunately, the apprehension and doubtful thoughts reappeared. I was very excited that I was about to marry the love of my life, yet apprehensive because of the same fact I was excited about.

It pains me to have to verbally express 'these thoughts' after experiencing such blessings from an awesome and faithful God, but as I'm committed to being transparent and honest in relating my story and journey for the benefit of those persons who can relate to it, here goes….:

(1) Suppose Doyle decided after we were married that he didn't love me anymore?
(2) How will I deal with the sexual part of the marriage given my sexually abusive background?
(3) What if I got tired of him, then what?
(4) What if I couldn't remember the vows on the day and all the plans go awry?

I knew that these thoughts were lies from ''The Father of Lies'', Satan himself, so I decided to pray and fast about them with intentionality, every step of the way during the execution of the plans. God came through for me yet again, and the life changing day arrived.

I had told Doyle that since the wedding was taking place in the morning, I didn't want anything to eat. However, being the loving, responsible and thoughtful man he was, it wasn't hard for him to be convinced by a Restaurateur to provide breakfast for me and my bridal party. Let's just say, I arrived late for my wedding because of breakfast.

However, the day flowed beautifully, and I wasn't even perturbed when our photographer discouraged me from using the beach as our backdrop. It had rained that morning, and the water was brown. Walking by faith, I confidently told her, "I am going to take my photos by the beach as I had planned, and the water will be blue." Guess what? True to my faith and prophetic declaration, the photos came back, and the water was beautiful and blue.

Our wedding was a blessing, and our honeymoon was beyond my expectations, as Doyle and I gradually got to love and know each other more. God is indeed faithful.... Why was I worried again?

Encouragement #9

- Always be prepared for Satan, the ''Father of Lies'', to attempt to derail you, using your deep-seated vulnerabilities for which you are still being processed as you obey the Holy Spirit of God.

- When you become aware of Satan's subtle and destructive attempts, go to the Lord with fasting and prayerful intercession. Be intentional, specific, confident and steadfast in what you are asking the Lord for, and pray expecting the breakthrough.

- Let Jeremiah 29:11-13 (these verses were already mentioned above in Encouragement #3) be your anthem and focal point of reference during this time of attack, and even afterwards.

Chapter 10

I was married......, now what?

We were blessed to live in a picturesque apartment complex and had great neighbours. The fact that we got to rent this apartment was a sheer miracle. Let me recap, we had started house hunting a few weeks before our wedding, and when we went for the viewing of this apartment, we realized that quite a few persons were also interested.

While one interested person was ardently engaged in negotiating with the Real Estate Agent, Doyle and I took the opportunity to slip upstairs, and there we held hands together, and declared to the Lord that the apartment would be our new "home", and we seal it with an embrace before the Lord. God answered our declaration, and we moved in partially because all our furniture did not arrive in time. We allowed ourselves to be content in our circumstances because we had each other.

As husband and wife, we visited many new places, and met new friends. I had to work hard at first to get used to being called "Mrs. Kidd-Mighty" or "Mrs. Mighty". Mr. Mighty promptly took me to get my passport amended to include my new name ...his name. (smile)

We were so very grateful to God as our new chapter of life together as husband and wife had started, however, as the days, weeks and months passed, our "masks", started to fall off, especially mine. I recall while I was in Sunday School, Sharon Earle Brown had aptly shared that when two persons are dating, they put their best foot forward, but they also inadvertently wear masks, masking their bad traits. That statement came back to haunt me as true, as reality hit me, in particular. I had taken "my baggage" into our marriage, and this caused me so many issues. Doyle became very frustrated at times because of my super sensitivity, insecurity, jealousy, unfair expectations, excessive demands on him for things that only God could give. I craved confirmation of his love constantly, and this added to his frustrations.

My troubles continue to heighten because I didn't like doing household chores, since, while living with Aunt Velma all these years, she did most of them. So now that my life and expectations had changed, I wasn't coping well at all. I accepted that I was thoroughly spoilt. I just didn't like housework in any shape or form, and I wanted and needed someone to do it for me/us. I had a genuine health issue with washing, as I was easily bruised. For example, my wrists would bleed when I did laundry, and I later found out that it was a reaction to the washing detergents I used. Before getting married I had indicated to Doyle that we would need a washing machine but that didn't come to fruition immediately.

The situation became untenable as housekeeping was not going well, and so anxiety, depression and a general state of unhappiness became a major problem for me/us. I just believed that I wasn't a good wife to Doyle, and it didn't help that my Aunt Velma kept calling me to ask if I was doing the very same things that were causing my distress. I attempted to include Doyle in my plans to address the situation by creating a Roster, but sadly he wasn't in agreement with that idea, pointing out that his stringent work schedule didn't give him enough flexibility to do those additional activities.

Thank God I got a ray of hope at our 6- months post counseling session. In the session Pastor Shimhue asked us how things were going. I shared the positive parts and bemoaned the negatives. He wisely said it was nobody's business how and when we did our chores, and I could pace myself as we dealt with them.

When Doyle shared my demand on him to constantly confirm his love for me, the Pastor encouraged him that females need more reassurance than males and he was to be a little more patient with me. He encouraged us otherwise, and I sighed with relief, as I realized then that I wasn't a bad wife after all. We decided to get a Day's worker to assist with the chores, and I started enjoying experimenting with cooking new dishes.

By the time my book is published I would have been married 23 years. Doyle has proven to be a loving, kind, patient, wise, true and helpful 'Priest' of our home, and a husband, father, mate, lover and friend. He is the calm in my emotional earthquakes and tsunamis. He quietly listens to my emotional volcanic eruptions and lovingly shows me another perspective. Tearfully I would concede, sometimes reluctantly, but I knew he was right.

Doyle tried his utmost best to give and show me happiness in the way he treated me and demonstrated his unwavering love for me, but there was still "an empty space" in my mind and spirit. I still felt like I was drowning at times, even with his love and reassurance. I had extreme emotions and habits ranging from always being active 'doing and feeling things' (like Martha in Luke 10:38-42) to be regarded as 'perfect', and at other times desiring to just focus on the Word of God (like Mary in the said book and chapter). I was totally out of control of my emotions in these moments, and at times I would bring on headaches (don't know how I did it), blame myself for mistakes I did not make, and relive bad incidents. I simply wanted to die, I was in a box that I couldn't come out of, didn't know how to get out of it, and wasn't sure how and where to get help.

I didn't share all these feelings with Doyle because I knew it was all my doing, and I didn't want to scare him that he had an unwell wife. You may be wondering if I shared my sexual abuse with Doyle? Yes, before we were married, I had shared my sexual abuse with him, and he comforted me by reassuring me that this didn't change the way he felt about me.

I walked around with a mask and talked and laughed with people, but I was drowning, I wasn't coping. At times I would be laughing and just as if someone snapped their fingers, I would change and be upset, tearful, angry, hurting and unreachable. These mixed emotions and behaviours caused my family and friends to avoid being around me.

I recall one occasion when Doyle and I were enjoying a walk, and I just snapped, lashed out at him and stormed home leaving him. When he got home, he told me he wanted to talk with me. I dreaded the talk and had my barriers up, knowing what was coming.

He was understandably hurt and embarrassed, so when he told me how frustrated he was and how he was having thoughts of being separated from me because of the uncertainties and frustrations from one moment to another. My barriers went down, and the reality hit me square in my stomach. I was by now feeling ashamed, guilty and condemning myself. I apologized profusely and promised that I would be 'better'. Then and there it dawned on me that I could not personally make myself better, only God could do that to and through me. Doyle accepted my apology, and we both moved on with me making much effort to adjust my ways, and he trying to endure my less frequent 'snaps'.

It was a hard time and struggle for me to control my emotions despite my valiant efforts, and one day I had reached my limit, and decided that I was going to end it all. Yes, suicide became the best option, in my view. I was scared, but still started to think of the easiest and least painful way to go about doing it.

Crying profusely, I headed for the bathroom to swallow a bottle of pills, but, as I was heading there, I felt like "a force" pushed me back into the bedroom. I found myself on my knees by my bedside, bawling out to God. I cried so much I thought I was indeed going to die. I remember saying to God: "I can't do this on my own any longer God, this is not the *'me'* you created. P...l...e...a...a...s...e help me, save me from myself." I kept sobbing and crying out to God, and soon I started to experience some peace and comfort in my body, soul and spirit. I wish I could tell you that everything changed immediately but I can't, because it has continued to be a process. Fortunately, I don't struggle with suicidal thoughts anymore, but sometimes I still get frustrated and angry. I started to ''speak life and positivity'' over myself, manage my thoughts more intentionally, and relied on God more and more for strength and guidance. I realized that over the years as I did these things, I gradually became more mature in my Christian walk, and more experienced in how I handled the occasional negative moments. God is still working on me as I am only made perfect through Christ.

My life wasn't only always etched with trials.

I enjoyed ministering through drama, dance, teaching Sunday school or just having good fun at a Sunday school picnic or trip. Let me share more secrets with you, I dream of writing, acting and directing with Bishop T.D. Jakes & Alex and Stephen Kendrick. I was so serious about it that I tried to contact T.D. Jakes and was told by someone in his office that he uses a company to do casting for him. After being ministered to by watching the film "War Room", my excitement grew to the point where I sent an email to the Kendrick brothers asking them to film a movie in Jamaica. However, I didn't get a response.

I have also had some great and transformational times in my marital relationship. Doyle and I ensured that we synchronized our vacation leave times so that we could travel or just spend those times together. He is what is referred to as "a real trooper", and I remember a few times when, even though he wasn't a member of our Church's Drama Group, he came to our rescue when we were at out wits end trying to resolve some unplanned for disappointments.

One occasion worthy of mention here was when we had the 8th Caribbean Baptist Fellowship Youth Festival in the Bahamas in the year 2009. Doyle played the role of my 'villain boyfriend', because the appointed actor wasn't attending the Conference. This role called for Doyle to dig deep to perform, and with the help of God we ministered together well.

Doyle has always supported me in almost all aspects of my life during our marriage, in big ways and small ways, and this has always been a blessing to me. His love for me is without question, and I'm so grateful that God has placed him in my life when He did. He is my constant friend amidst all my struggles and bad moods.

We also worked together in ministering to couples who are planning to get married, including couples formally engaged and those who are newlyweds. We serve and bless "the needy" in so many ways, and we visited the sick and the elderly.

At two (2) of the saddest moments of my life, when my father, "dada", and Aunt Velma died. Doyle was very supportive. He was also there for and with me in the years 2017 to 2019 when I experienced a traumatic time with severe medical challenges.

When I was hospitalized in 2018 in a very serious condition to the extent of having to get blood transfusions, he visited, "laid hands on me", and prayed over me every day.

For my part, being in the hospital didn't stop me from praying for those around me or me ministering to them. I give God thanks that as I poured out into other people's lives, my praying friends at my new church, Transformed Life Church, Doyle, and other family and friends, prayed for and poured into me during that 'testy time' of my life.

At the beginning of Chapter 2, I mentioned an experience I had while undergoing a medical procedure, and I now elaborate on that procedure and circumstance.

About a week after being discharged from the hospital, I had to return there to complete a "pipelle procedure", as was described before. As I lay on the bed experiencing such excruciating pain, and the doctor and nurse performing the procedure, I had a flash-back over my life: I recall thinking:" Why Lord, why yet another pain," I thought, as I struggled to hide my tears but not my pain.

When the procedure was finished, I had to push aside my pain to assist my nephew, Keneil, who had an appointment at the hospital that same day. He was diagnosed with cerebral palsy at birth.

One of my major hurt, pain, disappointment and shame, which I will share with you reader, is that of not being able to bear children.

In the year 2018, Doyle and I would have been married for eighteen (18) years, but we didn't have any children. This was a source of pain, doubt, shame and disappointment for me. Doyle was hurting too, and we talked and prayed about it quite often. I wanted to have children so much, in fact, we believe that God gave us the names of three (3) children that we would have.

With this belief in mind, before each menstrual period I would dread the outcome with doubt and fear whether or not I would be pregnant on each occasion. My dreams and hopes were dashed at each period, and I was always in a state of disbelief and disappointment especially when Mother's Days were being celebrated. Yes, we did several tests and tried medications and procedures, but to no avail. Strange as it may sound to others, I even had thoughts a few times that I heard God telling me that I was pregnant.

Breaking the Mold

While in the hospital, based on my age and the recurring presence of fibroids in my reproductive area, the Doctors recommended that I do a hysterectomy, that is, removal of my uterus. I told them absolutely not, because I believe in the promise God gave me that I would have biological children. I continued to hold on to the scripture in Numbers 23:19 where it says: *"God is not a man, so He cannot lie, neither a son of a man that He should change His mind. Does He speak and then not act? Does He promise and not fulfill?"*. He's faithful to perform what he has spoken.

Although I still have to deal with my doubts with God at times, I believe I will bear children from my body, because my God is a miracle-worker and can do the impossible!!

In 2010, the Lord told me that he has called me to *"Mothering"*. Not understanding what this meant in relation to my own biological child, I asked Him for clarification. During the waiting period for the answer, he gradually revealed to me that Doyle and I would have our biological child, as well as foster and adoptive children who would all be living with us in our home. He told me that it is not his desire for children to live in institutional homes, but with loving families. He said there were enough Christians in Jamaica to foster or adopt children. I was initially shocked about the call to *'mothering'* and the absence of the specifics regarding my own child, but over time I started praying about it.

I organized and started a Group called ''Children's Sanctuary'', in which spiritual women would meet up online, with me, to help me pray about this ministry to which the Lord was calling me. In the year 2019, a friend of mine, Holly Robinson, who was a foster mother (and eventually adoptive mother) at that time, told me about a Foster Program Initiative of our Government, which was operating through Child Protection and Family Services Agency (CPFSA), Family Life Ministries (FLM) and Nairn Family Home (In Canada). This initiative was called "For The Children" (FTC). Since Holly was so passionate about the welfare of children, she eventually became the Director of the program, up to her passing, sadly, in December 2021.

I was excited about this government-associated Foster Program, and after discussing it with Doyle, I made further enquiries about it. The next thing I knew is that we were completing the required forms to make formal application. We believe that this was the will of God, as we were also the first prospective parents to be interviewed for the Program. We went through all the processes, including home visits, police records, references etc., and on July 1, 2020, our five (5) years old daughter came home to be with us, as our family.

WOW!! The excitement didn't last too long before the dark thoughts started creeping into my mind, as reality hit home. Fear of how I was going to parent her, was I really going to be responsible for her, what if something happened to her while in my care, am I capable enough, can I give her the unconditional love she needs etc. All those thoughts bombarded my mind, but one thing I was sure of, no matter what....... we couldn't send her back to the home because this is our ministry to which God has called us, and we weren't going to fumble or 'drop the ball' so to speak.

The experience has been a rewarding, joyful and challenging teaching experience for Doyle and me. However, there were some serious challenges, primarily on my part, wherein my responses and learnt parenting style as treatment for some issues, were not the best for our daughter, and oftentimes I had to practice much self-control. Happy to say, however, the joy our daughter has brought with her cute and heart-warming smiles, the hugs, and yes!! prayers. These are treasures that will be etched in our minds and hearts forever. Yes, so many times she prays bible verses to Doyle and I. For example: ''Mommy, the Lord leads you beside still waters, He restores your soul, your cup overflows....." and so much more. I say with thanks, joy and gratitude to God, and to others, Look at our God!!

I have to speak the truth as many times as I can, to let my readers understand that the progress and break-throughs were oftentimes mixed with the dark thoughts, as, even as I mothered our daughter, I still considered myself as not being a bona-fide Mother because I was still awaiting my biological child, as God has promised me.

The Lord set me straight at a Workshop I attended, entitled ''Waiting on God's promises". During one of the sessions, the Holy Spirit reminded me, "your daughter is upstairs in bed, that is your daughter you asked for, stop waiting for "*a child*", and love HER!!" I immediately repented, because I knew that it was true; I was still consumed with waiting on *"the child he promised"*, believing in my own mind and heart that "biological" is what makes God's promise complete. I concluded that if God closes a womb, it won't be opened until and unless He deems it to be so or not so.

I am eternally grateful that God has entrusted "his" daughter to Doyle and I, and we are satisfied that it is according to His will. Yes, God gives us His desires and answers our prayers in His way and His timing.

Encouragement #10

- I would recommend pre-martial and a post-wedding counseling sessions for married couples, as it truly provided Doyle and I with new perspective on the wedding, the marriage, the expectations, the requirements and role of each person, and offer encouragement along the way. If your Church fellowship doesn't offer these two-tiered counseling sessions, you could try to initiate its introduction by discussing it with the Leaders.

- Assess your state of mind and health and allow the Holy Spirit to guide you in seeking help: whether telling a trusted family/friend or trained counsellor.

- However, if you are having suicidal thoughts, or thoughts of hurting yourself in any way, or hurting other persons, or if you are 'hearing voice' that are telling you to do things that are wrong, seek a trained/spiritual Counselor and a Church fellowship immediately!

- Ponder on and be conscious of what you are thinking about. If you see you are meditating on many negatives make a shift very quickly from that mindset by; meditating on God's word, singing or listening to a gospel song or reviewing a sermon that had a great impact on you before. These are actions to encourage you and help you to resist the subtle and deceptive attack of the devil.

- Believe and accept that You are perfect only through Jesus Christ. God isn't finished with you yet, trust the process of getting much closer and more knowledgeable about him while going through the many and varied trials. He's always with you, and he says in his words that his grace is sufficient to strengthen you and take you through it all.

- This is confirmed in 2 Corinthians 12: 8-10: (vs. 8) - *''three times I pleaded with the Lord to take it away from me. (vs. 9) - But he said to me, 'my grace is sufficient for you, for my power is made perfect in weakness, therefore I will boast all the more gladly about my weaknesses, so that Christ's power may rest on me. (vs.10) – That is why, for Christ's sake, I delight in weaknesses, in insults, in hardships, in persecutions, in difficulties. For when I am weak, then I am strong''.*

- Don't be caught up with ''The Promise'', thereby making it become ''your god'', and so forget the one and only ''true God'' who is both the Promise-Maker and Promise-Keeper'', who made the Promise. God packages his gifts and promises in ways that we aren't looking for, at times or in ways we may even consider a curse. Be opened-minded, and don't be afraid to tell Him how you feel. *In Isaiah 1:18 KJV), God says: '' Come now, and let us reason together, saith the Lord: though your sins be as scarlet, they shall be as snow, though they be red like crimson, they shall be as wool''.*

Chapter 11

Destiny Helpers

"**D**estiny helpers" are divinely connected to our destiny, in accordance with God's pre-destined will and purpose for our lives, their lives, and for the nations of the world. They don't have the power in themselves to help you, but they connect you to people who can, and whom God has also chosen to become involved. Some examples of whom they can be are:

- Angelic beings: Biblical example is the angel that visited Mary and told her that she would become pregnant and ultimately become the earthly mother of Jesus Christ, the Promised Messiah. Story outlined in Luke 1:26-38.

- The Holy Spirit, whom I have mentioned several times throughout my story. He informs, reveals, directs, and instructs me about things.

- Human beings, who can be family, friends, other persons whom God uses to grant us favours at strategic times and situations. They can either be strangers who God chooses to put on assignment in our lives, or whom the enemy uses to cause us hurt and harm (I will explain later).

I couldn't finish this book about my story and journey without highlighting some of the persons who have left an indelible mark on my life, and in my heart.

The very first destiny helper I want to salute is….. (drum roll)..... The Holy Spirit, without you I would have died already. Thanks Abba!!

The very next helper is Velma Dallas, *'mi madre'*. I have mentioned her as my dear Aunt Velma, but I must do it again. A more caring and faithful woman you couldn't find, licks and all. Aunt Velma single-handedly took full care of Sophia, my sister, myself, our cousins, and other children for short stints. She was selfless, often deprived herself of things she needed, so we could go to school or have other amenities. Most importantly she taught us about God, and she lived a life of focus on Him, and for his Purpose in her life and the lives of us all. Aunt Velma as ''dada'' stated, you didn't regret assisting me because I have been living out the good purposeful life God has called me to live. Thank you!!

Sarah Newland-Martin, though you are not alive, I am so grateful for your encouragement and listening ears at that Youth Fellowship Retreat when I was overwhelmed with my baggage and shared my heart. Thank You!!

Jacqueline Riley, you are my friend, but I consider you a sister from another mother. We met at approximately age 11, and our relationship has blossomed over the years like fine wine. We are aged just a day apart, have the same height, have many similarities but still so uniquely different. You speak into my soul and show me things that blindside me at times. You are truly a selfless person, friend and my sister...I love you. Thank You!!

Keisha Jarrett, thanks for being my friend through thick and thin. You are truly a gem and a true friend. Thank You!!

Millicent Daley -Miss Millie, you were very kind, compassionate and loving. You always had some delectable meal to offer, and your welcoming home in Mona, so ready to receive me when I came home from school, because Aunt Velma was at work. I remember the day I got in trouble in High school, and I chose you to represent me. You lovingly told me you couldn't do it, and you spoke to Aunt Velma for me. Thank You!!.

Charmaine Allen and Audrey (Sandra) Hudson, you were both like my sisters and were there to assist me as I navigated my late teens into adulthood. Charmaine you were my rock after I was raped, and you never blamed me. You helped me to 'breathe again' and was there when the tears weren't ready to flow, until when they were pouring down my cheeks. You helped to plan and organize my wedding. You are truly a rare soul, and I am ever grateful to you. Thank You!!

Sophia Richards Roper, we went through some rough times together: workwise, financially, relationally and spiritually. We were kindred spirits, inseparable and sharpened each other. Thank You!!

Grandma, Aunt Vie - You were a wise soul and your quiet deamour spoke volumes. You stood in the gap so many times for me and my siblings. Thank You!!

Pearline Clarke, my grand Aunt, you provided your home as a haven for me to spend holidays, vacations, and whenever I please. Our first meetings were very tense because we weren't connecting and adjusting well enough, however, as our times together increased, our relationship blossomed like fine wine. Your delectable meals were hearty and nutritious. It was a privilege and an honor for me to assist with caring for you in your last phase of life on earth. I truly miss you. Thank You!!

Doris Chisholm, you were not only Aunt Velma's friend, but also a tower of strength and great help for Doyle and I during our wedding planning stress. You were kind, caring, encouraging and shared yourself and what you had with us.

We are so grateful to you for these kind and generous acts. Thank You!!

Lisa Bell, Lisa, Lisa, you have been a friend, Counselor, encourager, Mother-figure, Boss, and a positive influence on me from the day I met you. Even before you became a Christian you epitomized the charge and belief of the passage of scripture in *Philippians 4:13, "I can do all things through Christ who strengthens me"*. You have such a heart filled with love and goodness, and I admire you and your family, who sacrificially treated up to 200 inner city children every Christmas.

Lisa, you helped me to see that it wasn't and is never about me, when I visited Aunt Velma the day she died. Thank You!!

A bit of reflection here.......... The day before Aunt Velma died, Aunt Velma, Shadeen, Sophia and I were at Sophia's home. Aunt Velma was giving Shadeen her recipe for her famous toto (a coconut dessert). Sophia had purchased Chinese food, but Aunt Velma wasn't interested in that menu. I instantly thought of sardine and white rice, mentioned it to her, and she said that's what she wanted to eat. Despite mentioning that meal, honestly, I wasn't up to fixing it, but Aunt Velma kept on asking, "Lulu guh cook di food nuh." (Lulu, please go and cook the food) I relented and cooked it, and she ate it with such relish like it was her last meal.

The next morning, I visited before I went to work, and when I saw my Aunt I saw death!! I told her goodbye, hid my tears from her and my sister, and left hastily. The image I saw of Aunt Velma's face and condition troubled me a great deal, and I broke down at work. A friend was asking me what was the matter, but I ignored him and dashed into the bathroom to cry. He was so caring that he sent another coworker to check on me, and I 'bawled' in her arms.

Lisa heard about my condition, came by my side and led me into a meeting room to find out what was wrong. I told her that I think my Aunt was dying, and if God took her, I was going to be upset with Him and not talk to Him. Lisa held me by my shoulders and literally shook me to get me to focus differently. She told me that the situation wasn't about me only, and that I was to be there for my sister. She also reminded me that God is God and can do as He pleases. Thank You Lisa!!

I realized the truth of what Lisa was telling me, so I repented, and by so doing, I was able to release my Aunt, so she could continue her journey home to her Maker. A few minutes later my sister called to inform me that they were taking my Aunt to the hospital. The next call I got from my sister was that Aunt Velma had passed away. Of course, the tears continued to flow in even measure. I was devastated but had more peace in my soul because I knew she had walked in the gift of salvation. It was a sad period and I cried until I thought I was going to die. Thanks be to

God that Doyle was by my side all the way, crying with me and providing me with support and comfort.

During my quiet time in His presence, the Holy Spirit revealed to me that God understood my state of mind and grief at my Aunt's death. He wants us to be honest before him about our true feelings, even when he is the target of our accusations and anger. He will wait for us to calm down and come to Him. I was believing that God would heal Aunt Velma, so when that didn't happen how I thought it should happen, I became upset, and very disappointed. My Aunt was dying!!!. It was only after her death that I learnt that death is also a form of healing and closure.

This verse in **Zephaniah 3:17 (NLT)** comes to mind, "For the LORD your God is living among you. He is a mighty savior. He will take delight in you with gladness. With his love, he will calm all your fears. He will rejoice over you with joyful songs."

God did just that, he calmed my fears and tears as I mourned my Aunt. He carried, comforted and reassured me with His songs.

I had previously spoken about **''Destiny Helpers''** in the category of humans who meant no good to me. These persons I will label ''Antagonists''. They were very unkind and abusive to me in one way or another, they hurt me, made my life very hard and miserable, and really disliked me.

At the time of the incidents, I hated them, wanted to take vengeance, I was unforgiving, bitter and unloving. Now, as I am writing, in tears, I can boldly and confidently say to you all, I'm at the place in my heart to forgive you all, not only to release myself in obedience to Jesus' command, but also to bask in his love and forgiveness, for myself, and to release you all from my heart, and mind and spirit. I send and speak love to you all, and to your families. Your ''works'' forced me to seek God as my true source to deal with my hurts, and this has caused me to further and better understand what Joseph said to his brothers in *Genesis 50:20, "You intended to harm me, but God intended it all for good. He brought me to this position so I could save the lives of many people."* Your actions towards me were all part of God's design for my life, in accomplishing my divine purpose. I can now talk about my sexual abuses and pain and encourage other hurting women. If I can get pass these hurtful pasts you my readers all can do the same with God's help. So, I say to all of you my ''antagonists'', Thanks!!

Prayer Partners, there are so many of you, but forgive my lapse in memory if I don't mention your names at this time. Charmaine Walker, Janice Rodriquez, Dawn Johnson, Andrea Hunter, Andrea Reid, Dawn Walker, Alicia Johnson, Jodi-Ann Johnson, Tracey Hyman, Michelle Williams, Natalie McFarlane, Avis Matthias, Lois Pinnock, Stacey Grant, Leonia McCoy, Kim Sophia Miller, Kenesha Simpson. Kimoy Callum, Shawna Kay James, and Marva Hansel. You are ALL my Purpose Driven, Expectant Crew,

God's Princesses, Discipleship Group members and friends. Thank You All!!

Gail Fraser, mi 'sista-fren', you have selflessly shared your heart, knowledge, family, home and friends with me. You are a grand networker and I enjoy your famous tea parties. Some of the things I admire about you are: your encouraging spirit, your quest for self-improvement through hungering for more of God, and your resourcefulness. Thank You!!

Yvonne Reid, you are my unique, priceless friend and 'Sista'. I have learnt so much about myself, God, and life generally, from you. As you always say you are keeping it real, you are truly authentic. You have made God your heartbeat, and that is precious. You said I was instrumental in your healing, but you had done the very same for me. Thank You!!!

Myra Wills, I already miss you so much, but the void will always exist because you are not alive to see and read my book containing the story of my life "through it all". You were such an inspiration, and I didn't take it for granted that God asked me to sit at your feet to learn from you. This shows that He had great confidence in you. We spent some wonderful time sharing and sharpening each other. We were kindred spirits as we were passionate about doing the will of God, no matter the cost. I will always remember you. Blessings to your family. Thank You!!

All you who have been mentioned are my prayer partners and my sisters in Christ, and I thank God for each one of you. You have not judged me as man judges, rather, as God the Father, through Jesus Christ says he judges, as the ultimate Judge of mankind. Many of you have been with me in some of the darkest times in my life. You have been patient, loving, encouraging, brutally honest, and true. You were placed in my life for such as the time that you entered. Thanks again!!

Dawn Maylor and Sherene Graham, you were and continue to be my honest, trusted, positive women of God, who were and continue to be my Assistants in various ways. You both are calm, strong, bold women who epitomize great faith in God and in his Word, and you have taught me how to activate the passage of scripture which says: "*I can do all things through Christ who strenghtens me.*"

Petra Earle Hutchinson and the three *'angelic'* Doctors. You ladies were very supportive and helpful with my medical journey, in my time of need. On reflection, I will now share in more detail my extreme medical challenges, and how the Lord provided much needed help for me.

It was during the period of one of my excessive bleeding stints during my menstrual cycle. I could or should have stayed home, and watch the service online, but I felt led to go to Church to praise and worship God, experience his rich presence in the community of believers, and hear the sermon preached – the Word given live!! I was still conscious of what was going on in my body, and as I pressed in.......pouring out praises and prayers to God, the bleeding intensified. I really wondered if this was how the woman with the issue of blood in Mark 5:25-34 felt.

As I sat in church, I felt the urge to go to the ladies' room, but Abba (the personal name for God the Father) prompted me to just sit in His presence until church ended, which by that time was fast approaching. I so wanted to disobey because of the discomfort I was feeling, and what I knew and feared would happen when I eventually got up. The urge to sit still overcame the desire to get up, so I stayed and worshipped.

The Church service ended, and people started to leave. I was still pressing into God in prayer, and then I felt it, the warm liquid gushing from my body unto the chair and flowing to the ground.

"Lord have mercy, I thought, not here, not on the newly bought chairs that so beautifully adorned the church's ambience and setting" It was then that I saw Petra, whom I knew, and was so glad to see her. I beckoned to her, she saw my stricken face, and rushed to me. If I never believed there is a true and living God before, I believed it in this instant. MY GOD had strategically placed Petra whom I knew, and not one or two, but all of three medical doctors who were behind me!!! These three (3) doctors didn't just happen to be there talking to each other, they were divinely placed there by My God "for such a time as this" (Esther 4:14).

I can't remember all the details, but I do remember that Petra made an alarm and got the attention of the three doctors. They saw what was happening to me and encouraged me to go to the bathroom with them. Petra assisted me to the bathroom. The doctors were trying to get all the information they could so they could assist me properly, as I was very weak, and the blood kept on flowing.

After getting pertinent information, they asked if I needed help and encouraged me to get to the Hospital's Emergency room. One (1) of the doctors, Dr. McAllister, took my contact details. I was able to transport myself to the hospital, and Petra accompanied me, but driving her own car. She was a real trooper, she took charge of everything to ensure that I got attention quickly, including demanding a parking spot for me near the door to the emergency section, got an Orderly to provide me with a wheelchair, took my medical and payment cards, and got me registered to see the doctor on duty. She contacted Doyle and never left my side until he came. Even after I left the hospital, she checked up on me, and Dr. McAllister also kept in touch with me. What can I say, God is faithful, strategic, on time, and just incredible. Thanks Abba, for these special women who were obedient to your call. Thank you ALL!!

As I type these words, I am saddened to say Petra passed away in late October 2023, after being admitted to hospital and battled for her life. She was there for me to help save my life, but she lost hers. I am deeply saddened by her passing, but I believe that she is safe and at peace and resting with the Lord. Her own story is a powerful one of defying the odds and she lived to experience the supernatural power of God. Blessings, strength, comfort to her family!!!

Abba, Father, I thank you for all these and other ''Destiny Helpers'' whom you have placed in my life. I pray this prayer for all of them and their families, taken from Numbers 6: 24-26:

> *"The Lord bless you and keep you;*
> *The Lord make His face shine upon you,*
> *And be gracious to you;*
> *The Lord lift up His countenance upon you,*
> *And give you peace."*

I also pray, in the name of Jesus Christ, for the gift of Salvation to be given to all those persons, and their families who are yet to accept Jesus Christ as Lord of their lives. That is the only gift that will ultimately give true meaning to their lives.

Encouragement #11

- No man is an island, and we are all here on earth not just for ourselves, but also to help each other.........a symbiotic relationship, even though sometimes the people whom we help, will not automatically be the ones who help us in return. Extend help anyway, from a genuine heart, as God looks at the posture of the heart, and the motives for extending help to others.

- When you feel like you are drowning, know you are not alone, and if you look beyond your pain, oftentimes you can see your ''Destiny Helper/s as 'a ray of hope'. Reach out, yes, reach out and accept and utilize your ray of hope, if I did it so can you!!

- Extend Love for your Enemies, you are only made perfect through Jesus Christ. In Matthew 5:43-48 Jesus was quoted as saying and commanding us to be good neighbours and to show love to our enemies: 43) "You have heard that it has been said, 'Love your neighbor and hate your enemy.' 44) But I tell you, love your enemies and pray for those who persecute you, 45) that you may be children of your Father in heaven. He causes his sun to rise on the evil and the good and sends rain on the righteous and the unrighteous. 46) If you love those who love you, what reward will you get? Are not even the tax collectors doing that? 47) And if you greet only your own people, what are you doing more than others? Do not even pagans do that? 48) Be perfect, therefore, as your heavenly Father is perfect.

Chapter 12

This is not the end but the beginning

It is such a sad thing to hear the appalling stories women who have been sexual abused have shared with me. Why have they shared with me? you may ask. Well as I have shared in my story, I have not kept quiet, God has used my pain and abuses as a platform to touch other hurting women. Every time I open my mouth and speak about one of my painful experiences, lives have been changed. It is easier for me to say to someone hurting, I understand what you are experiencing, because I have gone through it all: I have felt the pain, the fear, the shame, the insecurity, the doubt, the anger, the bitterness, the un-forgiveness, and the evil and dark thoughts. But for; the love, grace and mercies of God, the love of a wonderful and chosen-by-God husband, a beautiful daughter, loving, faithful, trusted family and friends, a church family, even ''Antagonists'' who served God's purpose for my life and journey, and so much more blessings, I would have been a total wreck today.

Like Joseph I can confidently say, "You intended to harm me, but God intended it all for good. He brought me to this position so I could save the lives of many people." Genesis 50:20.

That day that Uncle Basil saved me from drowning was much more than that. My merciful Abba kept His word in Isaiah 43:2:

> *"When you pass through the waters,*
> *I will be with you;*
> *and when you pass through the rivers,*
> *they will not sweep over you.*
> *When you walk through the fire,*
> *you will not be burned;*
> *the flames will not set you ablaze".*

God through Uncle Basil pulled me out of deep water that day, a water for which is symbolic of God working through him to pull me out of 'troubled waters', 'miry clay of struggles', 'hurt', 'pain', and setting my feet on solid rock with His saving grace. As He saved me that day and other days, He can save you too.

As I shared in Chapter 6 that the Holy Spirit said I was great and would be on television, well God keeps His promises. On Thursday October 26, 2023, the Director of For The Children (FTC), Mrs. Karen Fraser Williams, asked me to represent other FTC parents on the Kerlyn Brown's program ''Inspire Jamaica'' on CVM television.

Through this interview which was first aired in three segments on October 29th and November 5th and 19th, 2023, God used my pain of closed womb to provide hope to others in the same struggles. Listen, there is a way to fill your heart, arms, lap, home with children, you can do so through fostering as well as adoption. Ultimately there is a person who can fill your heart and provide peace, His Name is Jesus Christ our Lord and Saviour.

Through the televised interview, God also provided me with this unique opportunity to market *'this'* book even before it was published while I encourage women who have or are experiencing sexual abuses. He told me to go to the interview and open my mouth and he would fill it and He did exactly that. What a Mighty God we serve!

This is evident and evidence that when we are obedient and surrender to the will of God, He takes care of every aspect of our life.

This has been my gift to you my reader friend, my story of pain, hurt, shame, disappointment, self-defeating thoughts, repentance, forgiveness, encouragement, hope, sharpening and reliance on God. Re-read the encouragements after each chapter to help propel you into your purpose. If I broke the Mold and I am living a life of healing, you can do so too, because "You can do all things through Christ who strengthens you"!

I am so excited for you and would love to hear about your transformational story and journey. Don't give up when the battle gets hot for this is not the end but the beginning of a beautiful life of metamorphosis from caterpillar to your flight as a beautiful butterfly.

Encouragement #12

- If you are unable to bear children and would like to be a foster or adoptive parent, then there are facilities (in Jamaica as well as your Country) that can help you to achieve this end. They can assist you also, if you choose to help in the welfare needs of children, in the form of counseling, teaching, medical/healthcare, financial donations etc.

- You are not a victim, you are victorious through Jesus Christ!

www.ingramcontent.com/pod-product-compliance
Lightning Source LLC
Chambersburg PA
CBHW071124090426
42736CB00012B/2009